RECOVERY JOURNEY

Step by Step Guide Into Research Based
Holistic Sex Addiction Recovery Workbook

Dr Fai Seyed Aghamiri

First published by Ultimate World Publishing 2022
Copyright © 2022 Dr. Fai Seyed Aghamiri

ISBN

Paperback: 978-1-922828-48-4
Ebook: 978-1-922828-49-1

Dr. Fai Seyed Aghamiri has asserted her rights under the Copyright, Designs and Patents Act 1988 to be identified as the author of this work. The information in this book is based on the author's experiences and opinions. The publisher specifically disclaims responsibility for any adverse consequences which may result from use of the information contained herein. Permission to use information has been sought by the author. Any breaches will be rectified in further editions of the book.

All rights reserved. No part of this publication may be reproduced, stored in or introduced into a retrieval system, or transmitted in any form, or by any means (electronic, mechanical, photocopying, recording or otherwise) without the prior written permission of the author. Any person who does any unauthorised act in relation to this publication may be liable to criminal prosecution and civil claims for damages. Enquiries should be made through the publisher.

Cover design: Ultimate World Publishing
Layout and typesetting: Ultimate World Publishing
Editor: Vanessa MacKay
Cover image: Lightspring4-Shutterstock.com

Ultimate World Publishing
Diamond Creek,
Victoria Australia 3089
www.writeabook.com.au

Dedication

I dedicate this book to God, my Lord and Saviour, Jesus Christ for accepting me into His family. Discovering my Heavenly Father who has been so dependable has changed the course of my life. I make a promise to our Father that I will assist Him in liberating all of my brothers and sisters from the shackles of addiction. Prayer, along with work will be a part of this commitment.

To the men and women that bravely allowed me to accompany them on their journeys. I am indebted to you for your courage in revealing your challenges. You have taught me so much about humanity, human suffering, and human victory, to you I also dedicate this book and my services.

> "Do not fear, for I am with you; do not be dismayed, for I am your God. I will strengthen you and help you; I will uphold you with my righteous right hand."
> **Isaiah 41:10 NIV**

Contents

Dedication	iii
Introduction	vii
CHAPTER 1: What is Sex Addiction?	1
CHAPTER 2: Your Triggers Identification and Your HALT	15
CHAPTER 3: Trigger Management Tools	31
CHAPTER 4: Acting in and Acting out Identify Your Acting in Behaviours	87
CHAPTER 5: Positive Self-regulation	101
CHAPTER 6: Breaking Denial And De-Shaming Oneself With Honest Self-Disclosure	115
CHAPTER 7: Self-Care Before and After Disclosure	123
CHAPTER 8: Phases of Sex Addiction Recovery	135
CHAPTER 9: Causes of Relapse After a Period of Sobriety	141
CHAPTER 10: Withdrawals	155
CHAPTER 11: Non-negotiable Rules of Recovery	163
CHAPTER 12: Things You Can and Cannot Control	197

CHAPTER 13: Spiritual Awakening 213

CHAPTER 14: Love and Lust 231

CHAPTER 15: Why Boundaries? 257

CHAPTER 16: Sex Addiction and
Other Health Conditions 289

CHAPTER 17: Recovery in a Nutshell 305

References 321

Services and Offers 333

Introduction

Our acceptance of sex and hypersexuality is at an all-time high. The graphic depiction of sexual behaviour in the media, demonstrates how sex has merged with mainstream society.

Similar to gambling, sporting events, or watching movies, sexual expression has evolved into approved adult entertainment. Internet pornography has grown into a billion-dollar industry. The availability, affordability, and realistic depictions of sexual behaviours in digital media leave no room for imagination. These cultural shifts, have expanded the acceptance and convenience of sexual rewards. The increased accessibility to sexually explicit materials and activities has revealed that some people have an inability to control their urges, which results in continued engagement in these behaviours despite the emergence of negative consequences or sexual addiction.

Dr. Fai Seyed Aghamiri

Most people who become sexually addicted have a history of traumatic or adverse experiences in their formative years, making them more vulnerable to addiction. Sex addiction is a complicated disorder that impairs executive brain functioning, which has severe adverse effects on individuals, their families, and consequently, the entire society.

This workbook aims to offer approaches that are not only based on research and science but also on holistic principles that can be effective during recovery.

Please go to this link https://tinyurl.com/PDFworkbook to download your PDF workbook.

CHAPTER 1

What is Sex Addiction?

A lack of control over sexual fantasies, cravings, and impulses is classified as a sex addiction. While sexual desires are natural, sex addiction refers to behaviours that are carried out in excess and have a negative impact on one's life. Sex addicts may change their activities to engage in sexual behaviours on a regular basis, unable to stop their conducts regardless of the consequences. These consequences similar to drug or alcohol addiction consequences, can impact physical health, mental health, personal relationships, finances, academic performance, and quality of life.

Sex Addiction Signs:
- Lustful fantasies or obsessive sexual thoughts.
- Excessive time spent thinking about sex or performing sexual acts.

- Engaging in sexual activities online or offline.
- Hiding porn.
- Feelings of shame or depression.
- Excluding other activities.
- Excessive masturbation.
- Engaging in risky or inappropriate behaviours.
- Escalating in compulsive behaviours over time (needing more and more stimulation or engaging in more risky behaviours to reach the desired arousal).
- Cheating on partners.
- Committing criminal sexual offences for some.

There are multiple terminologies that refer to Sex Addiction such as Compulsive Sexual Behaviours, Hypersexuality or Pornography Addiction. Sex Addiction is characterised as a compulsive desire to engage in sexual behaviours in order to attain the same type of 'high' or 'fix' as someone who is addicted to alcohol or opiates. One feature could be behaviour secrecy, in which the individual with the disease becomes adept at concealing their actions and can even keep the disorder hidden from spouses, partners, and family members.

Excessive compulsive sexual behaviours, such as pornography use and masturbation, among other compulsive activities, have been shown in studies to lead to addiction, similar to drug addiction. According to behavioural health experts, addiction hijacks the brain, and is referred to as a brain disease.

Sex addiction like other addictions is about:

- deception (lying),
- denial (about powerlessness over sexual behaviours or the addiction),

What is Sex Addiction?

- delusion (i.e., normalising the addictive behaviours and telling themselves that everyone is doing the same).

Acting out sexually commences with an initial lustful thought or image in the brain. In general, addiction is a relapsing condition that starts in the brain. Whether it comes from drugs, money, sex, or food, the brain registers all sorts of pleasure in the same manner.

Dopamine, a hormone that helps regulate the mood, motivation, and capacity to focus, is released when the brain experiences pleasure. Dopamine also plays an important role in memory and learning. When someone uses addictive substances like drugs or compulsive sexual behaviours, the brain is flooded with dopamine. This surplus dopamine enters the brain and immediately begins to alter the way their thinking functions. The addictive ingredient has now been identified as a source of pleasure. The brain memorises and learns which substance elicited the most pleasure as a result of the surge of dopamine. Too much dopamine in the brain, affects with another molecule called glutamate. These two hormones subsequently take control of the brain's reward system, linking survival to pleasure and reward. As a result, addiction has deceived the brain into thinking it requires a large amount of pleasure-producing substances to survive.

Like other addictions, sex addiction begins with deceit of oneself before moving on to the deception of others. It is easy to see how this develops when the brain is convinced that the fix is necessary for survival, at the same time as the addictive behaviours reinforce the habit. Addiction is thought to be caused by this bizarre chemical mechanism. Once the first automatic lustful thought or image is sustained and entertained, the chemical cascade commences in a sex addict's brain. Although the individual has little control over the first automatic lustful thought, how that thought is dealt with is what creates the difference in ongoing recovery or relapse.

Sex addiction not only starts in the brain; it also causes serious structural and biochemical damage to the brain. Some of these damages are:

Conditioning of the brain's reward circuit causing addiction. The tolerance for sex and lust escalates as the brain becomes increasingly conditioned. As a result, the brain's reward system is no longer triggered or finds pleasure by interpersonal interactions or intimacy. Instead, the more compulsive sexual behaviours are repeated, the more the brain adapts to them and identifies these acts as a primary source of motivation.

Decreased stress and anxiety tolerance. Addiction alters and diminishes how the mind reacts to stress and anxiety. Sex Addiction, rather than helping individuals cope with difficult challenges makes the addict feel more stressed and overwhelmed in the long run. As a result, the addict will have a larger urge for the fix. If the cravings are not gratified, addiction can reprogram the brain to create negative emotional responses (e.g., anxiety, resentment, fear, etc.) in order for the person to give in and act out sexually.

Some recovered sex addicts will frequently have an odd new feeling of anxiety when they no longer feel the previous anxieties they experienced during their active addiction. In other words, they feel anxious for not being anxious. This is the addicted brain's approach of tricking individuals into having negative emotions so that it can get the fix it needs. This is comparable to a tantrum-throwing toddler who has discovered that by throwing hissy fits, their boundaryless caregiver would give in and succumb to their unreasonable demands in order to keep the peace.

Impaired brain areas responsible for decision-making, impulse control, and emotional self-regulation. The last region of the brain to mature is the prefrontal cortex which is in charge of planning, thinking, solving problems, making decisions, and exercising self-control. As a result, the younger a person is when they indulge in repetitive sexual behaviours (such as porn watching and masturbation), the greater the risk of addiction and vulnerability to this type of brain harm. Compulsive sexual behaviours and preoccupations can alter the brain stem, which controls daily activities such as heart rate, respiration, and sleep.

People who have trouble making good decisions, controlling their cravings, and regulating their emotions and behaviour are considerably more likely to repeat addictive patterns as a habitual maladaptive coping technique.

When compulsive sexual behaviour is stopped, the compromised brain areas may cause withdrawals and increased relapse impulses. However, the less unhealthy habits are repeated, the easier it becomes to stay sober due to the brain's reprogramming power and strengthening of previously weakened regions. It is apparent that addictions work in the brain in the same way that diseases do.

It has been established that sex addiction, like other addictions, is a brain disorder centred on the brain and its weaknesses, as well as the underlying neurology. It should not be viewed as a moral problem based on specific behaviours.

Regrettably, most addicts, particularly sex addicts, are stereotyped as simply having a moral flaw. Many people have negative stereotypes about sex addiction. It is crucial to acknowledge that these attitudes and judgments may make it more difficult for a sex addict to seek therapy and help. When addiction is recognised as a disease, such ideas and preconceived notions are radically altered.

Dr. Fai Seyed Aghamiri

What is normal and what is not normal?

When people come forward and claim their compulsive sexual behaviours are destructive because of their out of control nature and overwhelming functional and psychological impairment, the broader public reacts with rejection, stigmatisation, and condemnation of such individuals and their behaviours.

On the one hand, cultural attitudes towards hypersexuality (i.e., porn viewing and masturbation) are contradictory. There appears to be a sense of normalcy and tolerance in cultural attitudes, as if everyone watches porn and masturbates. To say certain activities, such as compulsive sexual behaviours are normal and unavoidable because everyone does them is a fallacy.

Not everyone can drink in moderation, and some people have allergic reactions or addictive tendencies, and that when exposed to alcohol, they can develop severe reactions or addictions. Sex and sexuality are gifts, and we have all been designed to use them to relate to, connect with, and become intimate with others. If your sexual behaviours do not take over your everyday life, relationships, career, or other duties, and you are not obliged to engage in them in order to function, you do not have a lust allergy or a sex addiction.

If you have developed an allergy to lust and you can recognise any negative consequences of your own porn viewing, masturbation, fantasies, or sexual activities with others or on your relationships and still can't stop, quit fooling yourself and get out of denial, your actions are no longer normal.

Sex Addiction Cycle: It all starts in the head

Sex addiction frequently follows a cycle (See figure 1. Understanding this cycle can help in figuring out how to break free. The cycle is divided into five (5) stages.

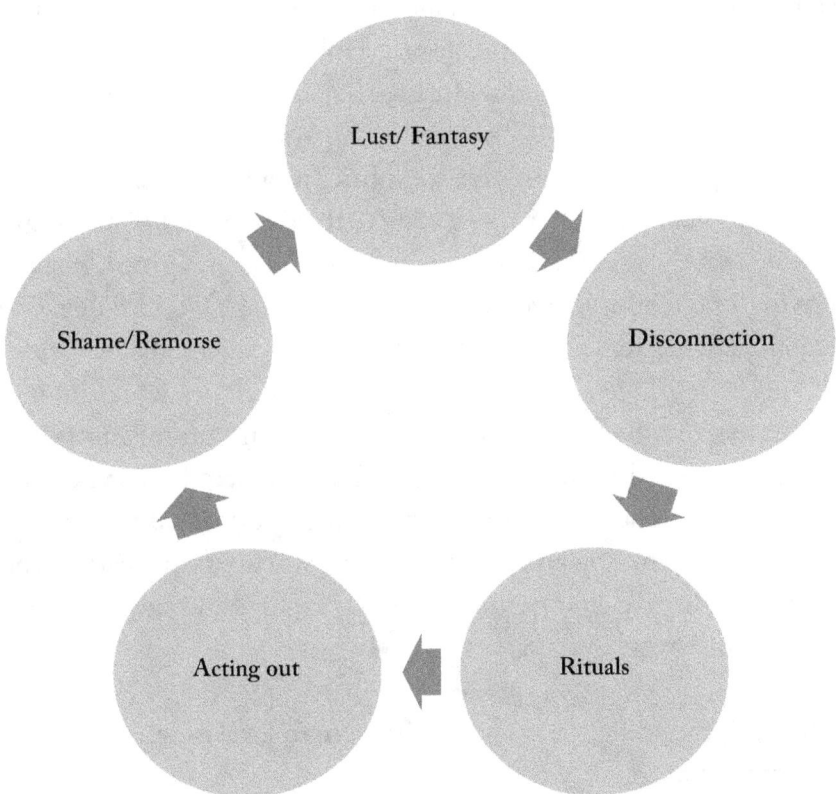

Figure 1: Sex Addiction Cycle

1. **Lust/fantasy** – either emotional or physical triggers operating as catalysts, causing a person to crave something that will make them feel better and can occur minutes before or days before acting out sexually. Lust and fantasies can occur as a result of triggers, or even serve as the initial triggers.

2. **Disconnection and cravings** –there is a strong desire to act out, as well as to mentally isolate and distance oneself from others (going into their own bubble). Furthermore, their perception of reality is now skewed and distorted.

3. **Ritual** – there is a predetermined plan or ritual (trance like state). For a sex addict, this stage provides the most intense rush and dopamine release. For example, looking for visual hits on the internet, or cruising around streets, shops, and other locations.

4. **Acting out**– feeling better for a brief moment before realising what has happened. For a sex addict, this is the end of the high, and it is rarely as satisfying as one had hoped or imagined, instead leaving one feeling powerless and unmanageable. Other negative emotions associated with this stage include despair and hopelessness.

5. **Shame/remorse** – feelings of 'I am bad' and promising not to repeat the acts dominate this stage. Remorse here is false because most addicts repeat shortly after repenting. Additionally, shame of not being able to stop and feeling of being worthless or a bad person obstruct effective change and can easily trigger another new cycle of compulsive behaviours.

Breaking the addiction cycle requires a high level of self-awareness and tenacity.

Addicts must identify, assess, and understand triggers in order to detect them as they occur, or better yet, before they occur. This task is especially important for addicts who can only stay sober for a brief time before relapsing. Failure to identify the trigger(s) or a relapse prevention action plan that does not effectively address those triggers are the most likely causes of an addict's cyclical pattern of constant sobriety - relapse pattern.

PRACTICAL RECOVERY TOOLS

I am going to burst your denial bubble and say:

- No, it is not normal to avoid intimacy with a real partner in favour of self-satisfaction through pornography, masturbation or seeking random sexual activities with strangers online or offline.
- No, it is not normal to be consumed with lustful thoughts and fantasies all of the time.
- No, lying to a partner or others while engaging in risky sexual behaviours is not normal.
- No, having sex with a partner while fantasising about an image seen elsewhere is not normal.
- No, needing to masturbate in order to fall asleep or deal with a mean boss is not normal.
- No, It is not normal to keep pornography or other sexual related activities hidden from a partner whom you know would be devastated to find out what you are doing in secret.
- No, it is not normal to feel shame after engaging in secretive sexual activities.
- No, lying, deceiving, manipulating, gaslighting and betraying your partner while blaming everything on their flaws is not normal.

- No, it is not normal to be unable to function sexually with a real partner while performing well with pornographic masturbation or random people.
- No, it's not normal to engage in so many compulsive sexual behaviours that you can't arouse sexually unless you intensify and escalate your sexual stimulations.
- No, masturbating while driving or at work is not normal or acceptable.

Anxiety management, numbing feelings, escaping painful aspects of life, mood altering, becoming vital to life, and at times being the most important need are all aspects of sex addiction. If this resonates with you then take the following test if you are curious that you may have an issue with sex addiction.

If you answer 'Yes' to 3 or more of these questions, it is recommended you speak with a trained sex addiction therapist to explore your responses:

1- Do you often find yourself preoccupied with sexual thoughts?

2- Do you hide some of your sexual behaviours from others?

3- Have you ever sought help for sexual behaviours you did not like?

4- Has anyone been hurt emotionally because of your sexual behaviours?

5- Do you feel controlled by your sexual desire?

6- When you have sex, do you feel depressed afterwards?

What is Sex Addiction?

(Based on PATHOS: A brief screening application for assessing sexual addiction, by Dr. Patrick Carnes was published in the Journal of Addiction Medicine: March 2012 - Volume 6 - Issue 1 - p 29–34)

Sex Addiction Cycle Questions:

⑦ Can you identify your own sex addiction cycle?

_____

_____

_____

_____

⑦ How is yours similar and/or different?

_____

_____

_____

_____

(?) Do you consider yourself a 'lust addict'? Explain?

_____

_____

_____

_____

_____

_____

(?) What part does lust play in your addiction?

_____

_____

_____

_____

_____

_____

What is Sex Addiction?

⑦ What do your rituals entail?

___

⑦ Do you recognise yourself in the shame and remorse stages of the sex addiction cycle? How?

___

CHAPTER 2

Your Triggers Identification and Your HALT

Thoughts and feelings that elicit a strong urge to indulge in an addiction are known as triggers. During recovery triggers are very common and expected. The addict has no control over the initial triggering thoughts or accidental visuals, but they have complete control over the subsequent thoughts, entertainment, and actions taken in response to those triggers.

Based on research a trigger is a stimulus that causes a traumatic memory to resurface. Triggers can drive addicts into fight or flight responses. Triggers can be caused by a variety of things, including distress and anxiety, and if they're not dealt with properly, they can lead to further cyclic distress and anxiety until the individual gives in and acts out.

A trigger could be any sensory recall of an event: a sound, sight, smell, bodily sensation, or even the time of day or season. A trigger for a sex addict could be an argument with their partner, driving through specific parts of town, a pushy boss, or remembering a traumatic event. Most sex addicts lose control of their sexual addiction when they are significantly triggered.

Triggered refers to having an emotional reaction to an upsetting situation. Sexual compulsivity and sex addiction are often triggered by a strong desire to escape unpleasant emotions, or a strong memory of earlier happiness obtained through lusty sexual fantasies and behaviour. Both types of triggers create a desire to act out sexually in sex addicts. When a sex addict is triggered, they often act out and engage in behaviours such as watching porn, sexting, visiting a strip joint, or sleeping with a prostitute.

Triggers can be **internal** or **external** for sex addicts:

1) Emotional discomfort, such as anxiety, tension, shame or any negative emotion, are examples of internal triggers. Thoughts, emotions, and feelings are all included in this category.

2) External triggers might include people, places, things, events, and stimuli in the environment.

In general, triggers include responses on a physical, psychological, and emotional level. Tightness in the stomach or chest, shoulder heaviness, and an apprehensive feeling throughout the body are some of the physical symptoms. Psychological or emotional symptoms

Your Triggers Identification and Your HALT

appear when triggers elicit arousal by simply entertaining lustful thoughts or recalling previous acting out behaviours, as well as planning the next relapse.

Sex addicts also have to deal with a variety of combined triggers. For example, if a person has an argument with their partner or has a difficult day at work (an external trigger), they are likely to experience emotional distress (an internal trigger), and the two triggers together will enhance the desire to act out sexually. Ultimately, visual cues such as seeing attractive people, sexual images on billboards, and other similar stimuli may amplify the sexual compulsive desires.

Not all triggers for sex addicts ought to be negative in nature. Closing a business deal, a new relationship, the birth of a child, material achievement, and experiencing happy feelings can sometimes elicit a reward and a drive to act out. Individuals must first learn to become aware, recognise and identify their personal triggers before they can learn to manage them.

Studies show that there is no way to avoid triggers because they are present at all times and in all places. Staying mindful and recognizing what triggers you and seeking to manage them as soon as possible is the key to breaking the cycle before it begins.

PRACTICAL RECOVERY TOOLS

'What was I thinking about, doing, saying, or feeling in the minutes, if not days, leading up to being triggered?'

Make a note of it. Pausing, paying attention and making a list will help you recognise exactly what triggered you and what emotional distress you're attempting to escape. This is how you practise mindfulness. The following table will assist you in identifying some of your triggers.

Your Triggers Identification and Your HALT

Examples of internal triggers:	Examples of external triggers:
1) Unprocessed anger 2) Shame 3) Resentments 4) Unmet needs 5) Feeling unappreciated 6) Unprocessed arguments 7) Boredom 8) Feeling Lonely 9) Fear 10) Anxiety, stress, depression or sadness 11) Unprocessed grief 12) Frustration 13) Feeling unloved and/or unwanted	1) Problems in the family 2) Financial challenges or gains 3) Arguments 4) Being criticised 5) Substance or alchohol use or dependence, gaming, gambling, and other types of unhealthy activities. 6) Accidental exposure to sexual stimuli 7) Unorganized solitary time 8) Negative encounters of any kind 9) Positive encounters of any type 10) Any type of unexpected life change 11) Holidays or solo travel 12) New Relationship 13) Relationship difficulties

Identify your own physical triggers:

⑦ People: father, mother, sibling, partner, friend, others. Your examples:

_____

_____

_____

_____

⑦ Places: car, work, bars, malls, gym, beach, others. Your examples:

_____

_____

_____

_____

⑦ Activities: conversations with partner, parents, friends, siblings, sports, watching movies, gaming, drinking, smoking, business trip, internet, phone, other. Your examples:

Your Triggers Identification and Your HALT

_____

_____

_____

_____

_____

Identify your psychological or emotional triggers:

⑦ Feelings: anxiety, jealousy, unworthy, shame, others. Your examples:

_____

_____

_____

_____

⑦ Unmet needs for validation or affection. Your examples:

_____

_____

_____

_____

_____

_____

⑦ Unprocessed and lingering resentments and anger. Your example:

_____

_____

_____

_____

⑦ Feeling unappreciated. Your example:

_____

_____

_____

_____

Your Triggers Identification and Your HALT

⑦ Shame, negative thoughts or trauma memories – I am not good enough, I am unworthy, I am bad, I must please others. Or other unhelpful thoughts. Your examples:

_____

_____

_____

_____

⑦ Situations: undesired occupation, financial difficulties, encounters with family members or those who are triggering negative emotions, others.

Your examples:

_____

_____

_____

_____

Identify Your HALT:

Self-care and self-awareness are required for life in recovery without relapse. HALT is a great simple tool to employ in this regard. This acronym serves as a reminder to take a moment to halt, pay attention, notice, and ask if you are experiencing any of the following feelings: Hunger, Anger, Loneliness, or Tiredness. These are all basic human needs. Unmet basic needs, can lead to cravings and relapse.

Hunger can be a physiological or psychological demand. Physiologically, meeting nutritional demands allows our bodies to function at their best, and we will continue to feel better. Psychologically, hunger can be linked to less tangible things such as affection, accomplishment, and understanding. Having a support system is essential in providing love and sustenance for the heart.

Anger is a misunderstood emotion, despite the fact that it is a natural and healthy emotion to experience. There are several ways addicts demonstrate their anger, explosion and or suppression (during active addiction), or expression (during recovery). The most essential thing is to HALT, pause, notice and take the time to figure out what's driving the anger and how to appropriately express it.

Anger, is associated with a lot of energy. Exercising, walking, reaching out to a safe person, pounding a pillow, and even cleaning are all active ways to get rid of the excess energy anger brings. Painting, meditation, praying, singing, listening to music, petting animals, and journaling are all creative projects that can help. Whatever approach is utilised to release anger, the focus must be on the reasons for the anger so that it can be released and expressed productively rather than destructively.

Loneliness can strike whether someone is alone or surrounded by a large group of people. Distancing from others and withdrawing out of fear or doubt can be self-imposed. However, when in the company of others, many people still experience an emotional sensation of loneliness. The longer a person is isolated and does not reach out for connection, the more difficult it is to reconnect. Because no one can truly recover from addiction on their own, support systems have been established as vital components of sex addiction recovery programs. Sex addiction thrives in isolation while recovery occurs in the comfort of connection and community. Boredom can sometimes be mistaken or even evolve into loneliness. Attending a meeting, engaging in recovery work, phoning a friend, paying a visit to a loved one, or reaching out and interacting with others can all be beneficial during this time.

Tiredness has a negative impact on the body, mind, and soul if it is not recognised and addressed. Reduced energy affects one's ability to think and cope. According to studies, going without sleep or being tired for an extended period of time has the same effect on the brain as drinking too much alcohol.

When the brain is tired and emotionally drained, it has a tendency to make poor decisions, lose physical agility, and forget key facts before shutting down on its own. As a sex addict's brain becomes more tired, they must rely on reflexes for survival. These reflexes are more likely to set off automatic compulsive behaviours as a self-soothing response. It is vital to meet the bodily need for sleep, rest, and rejuvenation to stay healthy and prevent relapses.

HALT Questions

⊙ Am I hungry?

_____

_____

_____

_____

⊙ When did I eat last?

_____

_____

_____

⊙ Was the food I ate nutritionally dense?

_____

_____

Your Triggers Identification and Your HALT

_____

_____

_____

_____

? Am I feeling angry?

_____

_____

_____

_____

? Who or what is the source of my anger?

_____

_____

_____

_____

? What resources can I use to express or reduce my anger?

_____

_____

_____

_____

? Do I feel lonely or bored?

_____

_____

_____

_____

? Have I reached out to anyone today?

_____

_____

_____

Your Triggers Identification and Your HALT

_____

_____

_____

⑦ What resources are available to help me prevent feeling lonely?

_____

_____

_____

_____

⑦ Do I feel physically or emotionally tired?

_____

_____

_____

_____

⑦ Have I done too much work and not had enough sleep or rest?

_____

_____

_____

_____

_____

⑦ What can I do to re-energize my mental and physical vitality?

_____

_____

_____

_____

_____

CHAPTER 3

Trigger Management Tools

Triggers are an inescapable part of the sex addiction recovery process. It is not always easy to predict when and where they will occur. Long-term sexual sobriety necessitates the ability to anticipate and prepare ahead for each type of trigger.

PRACTICAL RECOVERY TOOLS

Examples of some trigger management tools:

1) Leave the triggering environment/situation (Using 4 Ps).
2) Keep a journal to identify your triggers and emotions.
3) Rubber band technique.
4) Prayer.
5) Distraction, not avoidance, and the replacement of helpful thoughts for sexual thoughts.
6) Say STOP.
7) Recite your sobriety gratitude.
8) Engage in physical activities and have a cold shower.
9) Connect, reach out and talk it through.
10) Meditation or mindfulness practises.

As quickly as feasible, leave the triggering environment/situation.

Remember the **4 Ps** when it comes to your triggers, **P**ause, **P**ut down, **P**ass, and **P**ersist. Pause in your tracks, put down your phone, laptop, or other electronic device, pass and flee the situation, and remove yourself, or the trigger and persist in your trigger management activities. It's far easier to put out a fire and avoid becoming engulfed in it before it has ignited and gets out of control.

Trigger Management Tools

Sex addiction is characterised by out-of-control behaviours in which you lose control over lust, so stop putting yourself in a no-win situation, because even the smallest act of feeding your addiction will consume you.

Questions About 4Ps, Pause, Put Down, Pass and Persist:

⑦ What activities/behaviours do you need to start pausing since they could be triggers for you?

_____

_____

_____

_____

⑦ What difficulties do you face when pausing harmful behaviours, and how do you overcome them?

_____

_____

_____

_____

⑦ At what point is it still possible for you to put down risky devices or activities before relapsing?

_____

_____

_____

_____

⑦ Give examples of how and when you must pass (run from) your typical triggers in order to prevent relapsing?

_____

_____

_____

_____

⑦ What are your challenges when it comes to passing or running away from your triggers? What steps must you take to overcome them?

_____

_____

_____

_____

Trigger Management Tools

⑦ How convinced are you (on a scale of 0 to 10, with 0 indicating no confidence and 10 indicating extreme confidence) that you can persist in implementing the 4 Ps?

_____

_____

_____

_____

⑦ What P or Ps have you failed in the past when you relapsed?

_____

_____

_____

_____

⑦ What is your action plan to address it/them?

_____

_____

_____

_____

Keep a journal to identify your triggers and emotions and explore the anxiety or any other negative feelings you're experiencing. Instead of avoiding or numbing your emotions by acting out, learn to sit with them.

For effective journaling follow the steps below:

1) Pause and pay attention to yourself and your body.
2) Identify your feelings and where you feel them in your body.
3) Take some slow deep breaths.
4) Write 'I feel/felt………………..when…………………. because…….'
5) What is the message of the negative feeling(s)? Explore what are you disregarding, dismissing, denying or dishonouring within yourself for these feelings to emerge now?
6) Are there any positive lessons that the negative feelings are offering you? What are they?
7) How can you use those positive lessons to deal with the emerging negative feelings in a healthy and mature manner?
8) End your journaling with gratitude statements.

Example for Sitting in Emotions Journaling:

1) Identified feeling- Anger
2) Where in the body? In the chest.
3) Breathing.
4) I felt angry when my boss forced me to work overtime again because I am burnt out.
5) Anger is a sign that something has gone wrong. The message my anger conveys is that I have ignored my own boundaries and failed to tell my boss my truth.
6) The positive takeaway/lesson is that in order to stay psychologically and physically healthy, I need to create a respectful voice and express what I need.
7) By initiating a conversation with my boss about the hours I'm capable of working and setting clear boundaries for my own well-being I can use the positive lessons from my anger.
8) I am grateful for my family. I am grateful for my working body and so on.

Questions About Journaling:

⑦ What have I learnt in the last year about my sex addiction that I can write about in my journal?

_____

_____

_____

_____

⑦ What are the obstacles to me becoming my most effective self in my journaling?

_____
_____
_____
_____

⑦ When do I feel the most connected to myself and have the most time to journal?

_____
_____
_____
_____

⑦ What feelings am I suppressing and finding it difficult to express in my journal?

_____
_____
_____

Trigger Management Tools

⑦ Make a list in your journal of everything you're concerned about. Mark the facts that you are certain are true and not just a feeling?

_____

_____

_____

⑦ How can I find relief from the unpleasant realities of my life without acting out?

_____

_____

_____

⑦ Do you always end your journaling with some positive self-awareness and at least 5 things to be grateful for? Give specific examples.

_____

_____

_____

Rubber band technique

Addiction is a brain disease. Compulsive sexual behaviours activate the reward centre of our brain, which releases the chemical dopamine, providing a natural high for the individual. The neuronal pathway in the brain gets so strong over time that it becomes increasingly difficult to stop the behaviours. The rubber band method is a simple yet effective strategy to break problematic neuropath patterns.

The rubber band technique involves placing a thick rubber band around the wrist and snapping it against the wrist each time the wearer is tempted to engage in the unwanted behaviour. Snapping the rubber band causes pain, which prevents the subcortical, or impulse-controlling, section of the brain from rewarding the acted-upon impulse with a dopamine spike. The impulse-behaviour-reward circuit is effectively interrupted by developing the habit of snapping the rubber band in response to an urge (e.g., entertaining lustful thoughts and fantasies, wandering eyes, etc.).

Questions About Rubber Band Technique:

⑦ What do I do with my rubber band and in what situations do I use it?

_____

_____

_____

_____

Trigger Management Tools

⑦ When a rubber band is employed as an aversion technique, what happens in the brain?

_____

_____

_____

_____

⑦ What will happen if I use the rubber band every time I'm triggered for the next 30 days?

_____

_____

_____

_____

⑦ Is it acceptable if I use the rubber band for anything other than sexual compulsive behaviours? Explain.

_____

_____

_____

(?) On average, how many times each day do I use my rubber band for various triggers?

_____

_____

_____

_____

(?) What are the main reasons I use a rubber band?

_____

_____

_____

_____

Prayer

Praying is a beneficial habit to incorporate into your daily routine, and it is frequently encouraged by sponsors and people in 12-step recovery programs.

The healing power of prayer has been established by both scientific and medical studies. Prayers have been related to a decrease in activity in the parietal lobes, which process time and space orientation.

The language-processing areas of the brain (in the sub-parietal lobes) are more active in people who pray. Recovery is a full-scale war that demands exceptional commitment. Most people try to overcome their addictions by increasing their willpower or making promises to do better next time, but this rarely works. Finding or re-establishing a relationship with a higher power throughout recovery can be a huge aid on the road to long-term recovery.

The power of prayer in recovery, is another significant pillar that brings hope, motivation, and strength in the fight against addiction.

Praying can relieve worry, tension, and depression.

Praying can improve spiritual connection, increases dopamine levels, and improves mental focus.

Even if people do not believe in God, they can pray to whoever, or whatever they wish to be their higher power, as long as that power is greater than themselves. Consider prayer to be a dialogue between you and a higher power and talk as if it were a chat with a friend. Instead of waiting to feel like praying, just do it intentionally and daily.

Praying does not require one to be religious

Prayer is a mindfulness practise. Prayer is not a replacement for medical or psychiatric treatment, but there is accumulating evidence that prayer has beneficial psychological and physiological advantages. Carolyn Aldwin (2014) found that contemplative prayer helps with emotion regulation and physiological processes like blood pressure.

The calming effects of prayer may increase behavioural control. Self-care, exercise, prayer, and meditation produce happy feelings.

While texting and surfing through social media has the opposite effect. Members of Alcoholics Anonymous who repeated prayers after viewing images intended to evoke alcohol cravings reported experiencing fewer cravings than those who read the newspaper. In the MRI scans of those who prayed, the brain areas responsible for emotion and concentration were also more active. Additionally, studies have shown that while participating in group activities and journaling for oneself can make people feel good, praying is significantly more powerful. In a 2019 study involving 196 college students, those who read their gratitude journals aloud as prayers displayed higher levels of hope and self-actualization than those who simply read them to themselves or a peer. The abilities of empathy, perspective-taking, presence, and emotional control can all be fostered by prayer.

Both biological and psychological systems are active during prayer. Neurotheology, or the neuroscience of religion, seeks to comprehend the changes that religious experiences, and prayers bring about in our brains. Leading this enquiry is Andrew Newberg, M.D., a neurologist at Thomas Jefferson University in Philadelphia. According to Newberg, serotonin and dopamine are released when prayer inspires feelings of love and compassion. These two neurotransmitters affect how you feel in different ways. Your mood is directly influenced by serotonin.

Dopamine, is linked to motivation and reward. When a person is going through sex addiction recovery, they can no longer rely on the dopamine rush that comes from compulsive sexual behaviours. The greatest and healthiest way to replace these hormones is through healthy alternative practises like praying. According to Newberg, participants of a prayer and meditation retreat had improved levels of dopamine and serotonin, and these modifications weren't merely transient; rather, they produced long-lasting gains. Newberg reports that prayer and meditation can alter these neurochemicals in the brain permanently.

Prayer can also improve overall happiness if we define it as having meaning and deep relationships in one's life. The belief that there is something greater than one's everyday life and circumstances is the basis for praying to a higher power, and leading a meaningful life enhances overall good feelings. One's attention shifts during prayer from the pressing minutiae of daily life to the wider picture of what is significant. We make time in our lives for prayer and meditation so that we can communicate with a higher power or the universe outside of us and ask questions like:

How different would my life be if I got sober?

I know that perfection is impossible, so why do I insist on it?

What would it entail to be liberated from the urge to constantly be validated?

Examples of prayers to include into your recovery plan.

1) God/higher power, thank you for helping me to stay sober for another day. I pray for understanding of your plan for me as well as the ability to carry it out. I pray that you protect my sobriety tomorrow.
2) The Serenity Prayer- [God], grant me the serenity to accept the things I cannot change, courage to change the things I can. And wisdom to know the difference.
3) Eyes of Mercy- [Lord], look upon me with eyes of mercy. May Your healing hand rest upon me. May Your life-giving powers flow into every cell of my body and into the depths of my soul, cleansing, purifying, restoring me to wholeness and strength
4) Cleanse- I cleanse myself of all selfishness, resentment, critical feelings for my fellow beings, self-condemnation, and misinterpretation of my life experiences. I bathe myself in generosity, appreciation, praise and gratitude for my fellow beings, self-acceptance, and enlightened understanding of my life experiences– Lidia Frederico
5) Dear God, by faith I release all of these things into Your lap of grace, and I surrender to Your sovereignty. I cast all of my cares upon You, and I pray, 'Let Your will be done in my life today...'
6) Surrender-I surrender to you my past, present, and future problems. I ask You to take hold over every aspect of my life. I surrender to You all my hurt, pain, worry, doubt, fear, and anxiety, and I ask You to wash me clean. I release everything into Your compassionate care. Please speak to me clearly, [Lord]. Open my ears to hear Your voice. Open my heart to commune with You more deeply. I want to feel Your loving embrace. Open the doors that need to be

Trigger Management Tools

> opened and close the doors that need to be closed. Please set my feet upon the straight and narrow road that leads to everlasting life.
>
> 7) The Recovery Prayer- 'Today, I heal my body, my mind, my spirit, my life. Drugs are a part of my past; they are not part of my now, they are not part of my future. Today, I am clean. Today, I am clean and free. Today, I am becoming strong one second at a time, one thought at a time, one action at a time. I am learning how to live and to be the best parts of me today. Today, I am clean and free.'- Abby Willowroot

Questions about prayers:

⑦ Do I believe in the power of prayer, especially when it comes to managing triggers? Explain why?

_____

_____

_____

_____

_____

_____

⑦ Do I have any personal testimony about how prayers have helped me manage triggers?

_____
_____
_____
_____

⑦ Do you pray to anyone or anything, and how? Explain.

_____
_____
_____
_____

⑦ What led you to believe that you personally should pray to God or your higher power?

_____
_____
_____
_____

(?) Even if someone does not believe in the power of prayers, what would be the result of praying twice a day and when triggered for thirty days?

_____

_____

_____

_____

Distraction, and the replacement of helpful thoughts for sexual thoughts

Distraction, is a deliberate, active, and time-limited activity. Distraction is similar to taking a short break to re-energize and re-set the body and mind. In the long run, taking a break in the middle of a stressful circumstance (i.e., trigger), can be good because if this does not happen, the outcome will be burnout and acting out. In contrast, avoidance is a mal-adaptive coping method that helps to temporarily shut out uncomfortable emotions or triggers in order to avoid dealing with the source of the problem or finding a solution.

The brain of a sex addict is conditioned to become dysregulated as a result of unpleasant feelings triggered by intrusive thoughts or images. Triggers induce discomfort, and when the brain is stressed, stress hormones such as adrenaline and cortisol are released. These hormones can distort your perception of events, and possibly induce physical and emotional distress, prompting the addict to seek a fix to alleviate the suffering. In other words, a sex addict's brain has been conditioned to cause distress or discomfort in order to receive dopamine as a reward. The more a person succumbs to triggers and engages in the same compulsive sexual behaviours, the stronger the re-enforcement of brain neural pathways becomes. I always compare a sex addict's brain to that of an untrained puppy. The more you reward it because it keeps barking or for poor behaviour, the less it will obey you, and you will have less control over it. Doing something else, such as reading a book, cleaning, going for a walk, playing with the kids, or anything else that will completely divert the focus for a short period of time, is often enough to overcome a trigger.

Another cognitive behavioural therapy (CBT) strategy is replacing more positive thoughts for ruminations and lingering triggering thoughts. In the context of sex addiction, people usually recall just the glamorised features of earlier acting out when a trigger occurs. Focusing on replacing these distorted thoughts with actual reminders of the unpleasant things that generally occur following acting out can help with overcoming a trigger.

Counting backwards from 100 to 0 as many times as necessary is another simple but effective strategy for distracting and replacing a trigger or unwanted thought. Many people have found that doing mental math multiplication or subtraction while progressing to larger and more complex numbers has also proven beneficial. Distraction and the replacement of a sexual or triggering mental image for a picture of a partner or other loved ones (for example, on a phone) can also be effective.

According to research, our brains are continually striving to form habits in order to save time and effort. A habit, cannot be eliminated; it can only be replaced. The good news is that this is possible and achieved by returning to the beginning of the trigger or response cycle then sitting in the discomfort of not engaging in the old compulsive behaviour pattern and replacing the old response with a new one. Long-term sober people will attest to how challenging this intentional process was at first, and how it gradually became a more habitual habit.

Examples of Replacement of triggering thoughts with positive thought:

Triggering Thought	Replacement With Positive Thought
1) This is too difficult for me. I can never stay sober.	1) I'm not very good at this and that's ok. This is new to me, and I'm still learning.
2) I'm a terrible person and my family is better off without me.	2) I've made some poor decisions, but I'm still valuable. That's something I'd say to a friend or family member.
3) I made a huge blunder, and now I'm embarrassed since everyone will know about it.	3) I am a human being and not a perfect being. I understand that everyone makes mistakes. Tomorrow no one will remember this. This is something I can learn from because there are no mistakes, only lessons to be learned.
4) What's the point of trying. I have already messed up and might as well binge now.	4) No one promised that sobriety would be easy or painless. Rather than allowing one blunder to snowball into a full day of blunders, I consider this is only a minor hiccup that I can deal with. I wouldn't have known how to grow if I hadn't made some mistakes. Next time, I'll know what to do differently.

Triggering Thought	Replacement With Positive Thought
5) I am an unworthy, failure and inadequate.	5) I am enough; it is just my skewed and habitual thinking that makes me feel this way. At times the sobriety process appears to breakdown, but it could be the beginning of a breakthrough.

Questions about distraction, and the replacement of sexual thoughts:

⑦ Give some examples of using distractions rather than avoidance to deal with your negative emotions and sexual triggers.

_____

_____

_____

⑦ Give examples of how to replace negative thoughts and sexual triggers with positive thoughts.

_____

_____

Trigger Management Tools

_____

_____

⑦ How did you use avoidance in the past when triggered, and what was the outcome?

_____

_____

_____

_____

⑦ When you're triggered or having negative thoughts, do you ever question whether you're confusing a thought or a feeling with a fact? Explain and give example.

_____

_____

_____

_____

⑦ When you're dealing with triggers or withdrawals, what are your usual unhelpful thought patterns?

_____

_____

_____

⑦ And how can you distract or replace unwanted thoughts and feelings in a healthy way?

_____

_____

_____

⑦ What are your faulty thinking patterns when you've acted out in response to a trigger, and how can you modify them?

_____

_____

_____

Trigger Management Tools

⑦ Is it usual for you to exaggerate the significance of an unpleasant thought, feeling, or event? What happens when you do it this way?

_____

_____

_____

_____

Say STOP

When attempting to distract or replace triggers simply say stop out loud.

Stop what you're doing and interrupt your thoughts with the command 'stop!'

Take a breath and focus on your breathing. According to research, there is a correlation between how we breathe and how we think and feel. Breathing triggers several physiological systems that promote relaxation by striking the appropriate balance of oxygen and carbon dioxide in the blood. Slowly and deeply inhale, then softly and deeply exhale through your nose (counting to four for each inhale and exhale) while expanding your tummy.

Observe your own thoughts, emotions, and physical responses. What are the thoughts that come to mind? What emotions are present? What is the state of your body? Pay attention and spend a few moments with whatever comes up for you.

Plan and ponder mindfully about how you'd like to respond. What is your most essential and pressing concern? Instead of acting out, what is the next best action? Focus your attention and take one small step at a time. Continue to be cognisant of what you have in your sobriety toolbox and choose to incorporate it.

Questions About STOP:

⑦ When you're triggered, do you ever pause and consider the advantages and disadvantages of acting out? Explain.

_____

_____

_____

_____

⑦ What do you notice if you pay attention to your breathing when you feel triggered or uncomfortable?

_____

_____

_____

_____

Trigger Management Tools

⑦ Do you notice yourself breathing quickly, slowly, with difficulty, or holding your breath when you're triggered? Anything else?

_____

_____

_____

_____

_____

⑦ When you're triggered, how difficult is it to stop and pay attention to your feelings in the present moment?

_____

_____

_____

_____

_____

_____

? Do you find yourself anticipating the future rather than being present and appreciating the present moment?

_____

_____

_____

? Are you preoccupied with how things should be rather than accepting and dealing with them as they are?

_____

_____

_____

? How do you plan to use the STOP strategy to manage your triggers?

_____

_____

_____

Trigger Management Tools

Recite your sobriety Gratitude

Gratitude fosters contentment, and contentment is defined not by having everything, but by being grateful for everything you do have. Start a gratitude diary to keep track of your gratitude list and then memorise a few of your favourites so you can recite them when triggered. The gratitude list in recovery is quite effective. Gratitude inspires a positive attitude and outlook. It alleviates conflict and feelings of loneliness. Research shows that, gratitude provides physical benefits such as a lower heart rate, blood pressure, and stress levels. Experts in the field of addiction agree that gratitude can help a person achieve a successful recovery. It lowers the risk of relapse.

In recovery, a gratitude list is a written list of everything you're grateful for in your recovery and in your life. However, this is not a one-time task. A gratitude list is something that should be done on a regular basis. It may begin with the top ten things for which you are grateful, but it should continue to increase with each passing day. You should add at least one new item to your gratitude list every day.

Examples of gratitude

> I am grateful for my sobriety.
> I am grateful that I wake up with a clear mind.
> I am grateful for being in good health.
> I am grateful for my functioning body and organs.
> I am grateful for my supportive family.
> I am grateful for my fellowship.
> I am grateful for my relationships.
> I am grateful for my therapist, 12-step meetings, sponsors, and support groups to keep me going.
> I am grateful for my freedom.
> I am grateful for my career opportunities and the ability to work.
> I am grateful for my financial abilities.
> I am grateful for my humble attitude.
> I am grateful that I have the potential to make a difference in the lives of others.
> I am grateful that I can accomplish my goals without being held back by addiction.

Questions about sobriety gratitude:

(?) What do you have to be grateful for in your life?

_____

_____

_____

_____

Trigger Management Tools

⑦ Who are the people for whom you are grateful, and why?

_____

_____

_____

_____

⑦ What are some of your memorised expressions of gratitude that you can use when you're triggered?

_____

_____

_____

_____

⑦ In what ways do you incorporate gratitude into your daily routine?

_____

_____

_____

_____

(?) How and why may expressing gratitude be a good way to deal with triggers?

___

(?) Are you more critical and pessimistic about your situation than appreciating and optimistic? Explain.

___

(?) Is it possible to be grateful for your sex addiction? How?

___

Trigger Management Tools

⑦ What instances do you express gratitude in, and how often do you do so?

_____

_____

_____

_____

⑦ Spending time with loved ones is a great way to express gratitude; how frequently do you do this?

_____

_____

_____

_____

Engaging in physical activities and getting a cold shower

Studies have shown that physical activity can be a helpful substitute for addictive substances or behaviours, as well as an effective strategy to manage triggers throughout recovery.

Both exercise and addiction induce the release of feel-good neurotransmitters like serotonin and dopamine, which activates the reward circuit. Physical activity during triggers can have mood-enhancing effects, boost self-control, and has the ability to lessen withdrawal's intense discomfort.

Exercise can help you feel less stressed both physically and mentally. Tension builds up in our bodies when we are at work, during routine discussions, or even while we are watching television. This pressure can also be exacerbated by daily stressors. Movement helps you discharge any negative emotions you have been holding inside while also easing this tension. Focused exercise expends energy that would otherwise be used for unhealthy stress relief.

Exercise naturally and favourably alters your brain's chemistry. Exercise causes your body to release endorphins, which gives you a feeling of euphoria. It's the same endorphins that your body released when you were acting out. However, sexual acting out causes an imbalance that interferes with a person's ability to enjoy life and find fulfilment. By doing regular physical activity while undergoing therapy, you can replenish your body's natural endorphin levels. This not only lifts your spirits but also reminds your body that it has the power to regulate your mood and brain chemistry on its own.

Because we can benefit psychologically and emotionally from both practises equally, exercise and meditation have been equated. We can reclaim our consciousness and centre ourselves by moving. You might get an uplifted, revitalised, and rational feeling after exercising. Finding this clarity can make managing recovery much easier when dealing with the chaos of addiction.

Exercise has a perspective-altering effect. Exercisers report higher optimism and self-assurance along with lower anxiety and depressive symptoms. This occurs in part because your body calibrates and adapts itself while you exercise, but it also occurs because you feel

Trigger Management Tools

pride, worth, and accomplishment as you watch your body change, and your goals materialise.

Numerous studies have shown that regular exercise can accelerate recovery from addictions like substance abuse by 95%. These studies also show that exercise can help with the reduction of stress, anxiety, and depression, all of which can contribute to the emergence of addiction. Additionally, regular exercise promotes better sleep, more energy, and higher emotions of wellbeing. These benefits all contribute to a life that is much easier to manage and enjoy as well as a recovery that is more feasible and long-lasting.

Taking a cold shower once or twice a day can help ease depression. The first benefit of cold water is that it lowers inflammation in the brain. Inflammation has been linked to depression, and symptoms of depression can be alleviated simply by chilling the body down significantly. The second is that cold showers raise noradrenaline levels which effectively suppresses the depressive symptoms. Third, it may also aid by redirecting blood away from your extremities and towards the major organs, including the brain. That means the brain gets a lot more oxygen-rich blood, which helps it perform better. Cold showers also increase beta-endorphin levels, which reduce stress in the body and enhance homoeostasis, which includes pain regulation, behavioural stability, and reward.

Taking cold showers must be done slowly. By taking a regular warm shower and then gradually lowering the temperature.

In summary, cold showers may assist an addict in escaping the miseries of unpleasant triggers and post-acute withdrawal symptoms. Hydrotherapy was recommended to AA founder Bill Wilson in the 1930s as part of his addiction recovery treatment.

Examples of physical activities to manage triggers

1) Walking
2) Running
3) Swimming
4) Boxing
5) Hiking
6) Cycling
7) Gardening
8) Dancing
9) Aerobic exercise such as water aerobics
10) Resistance, or strength-training such as weightlifting, push-ups

Questions About Physical Activities:

⁇ What physical activities can you do to help you manage your triggers?

_____

_____

_____

_____

_____

_____

Trigger Management Tools

⁇ What difficulties will you face in doing so?

_____

_____

_____

_____

⁇ How can you overcome any obstacle to engage in some type of physical activity when triggered?

_____

_____

_____

_____

⁇ Have you tried engaging in some type of physical activity to address your personal triggers in the past? What was the outcome?

_____

_____

_____

_____

⁇ If both addiction and exercise stimulate the reward system and stimulate release of feel-good chemicals like serotonin and dopamine. What role do you believe exercise can have in trigger management?

_____

_____

_____

_____

⁇ How might exercising as a form of dealing with your triggers improve your self-esteem?

_____

_____

_____

_____

⁇ What are your top three exercises that you consider doing when you're feeling triggered?

_____

_____

Trigger Management Tools

⁇ What are your thoughts about taking a cold shower when triggered?

⁇ What are your feelings on taking cold showers on a regular basis?

Connecting, reaching out and talking it through

Reaching out to a mentor, sponsor, loved one, or friend and talking through the triggering experience can aid in the processing, overcoming, and prevention of acting out or the occurrence of the same trigger in the future. When most addicts are triggered, they isolate themselves, giving their addiction more chances to drive the bus. So do the opposite and reconnect. Addictions typically cause people to become isolated, it is critical to maintain contact with others while in recovery.

When faced with temptation, recovering addicts need someone they can call and feel secure enough to be honest with. Individuals must first admit that they need others, and then they must reach out to others and be honest in order to form accountability relationships. Recovery happens in the comfort of a community of people and can't be combated alone.

When triggered, attending additional therapy sessions and also 12-step meetings might provide further emotional and spiritual support. Individuals should not be afraid to make a pre-arrangement with some supportive people to send an SOS text message when they're triggered and need to connect. For some recovering addicts, this has proven to be a great tool for receiving rapid and immediate support during difficult times.

Questions About Connecting and Reaching out

(?) What does Fellowship mean to you?

_____

_____

Trigger Management Tools

_____

_____

⑦ When you're triggered, do you reach out to others?

_____

_____

_____

_____

⑦ Do you openly discuss your struggles and triggers with others?

_____

_____

_____

_____

⑦ What obstacles are you up against that prevent you from reaching out to others when you're triggered?

_____

_____

⑦ What are the advantages of reaching out when you're triggered?

⑦ Why, in your opinion, is it vital to reach out and connect as a method of trigger management?

Trigger Management Tools

⑦ When and if you are triggered, who can you turn to for help? Make a list of them.

_____

_____

_____

_____

⑦ When was the last time you reached out to someone because of a trigger? What was the end result?

_____

_____

_____

_____

⑦ Do you ever feel inferior or embarrassed when you need to seek help from someone? Explain.

_____

_____

_____

⁇ Are you planning to send an SOS text message to some supportive people if you're triggered? Explain.

_____

_____

_____

Meditation or mindfulness practises

Meditation is a deliberate practise that leads to increased consciousness. It is a sense of oneness that decreases stress and improves the inner faculties, creativity and efficiency. Meditation takes the individual to the deepest level of their inner self, and beyond the mind. According to studies, ninety-five percent of our activities are pre-programmed or unconsciously directed. Mindfulness is the total opposite of these automatic processes. Meditation is more like executive control than autopilot, and allows for conscious acts, willpower, and choices.

This requires time, patience and practise. The more the intentional brain is used, the more powerful it becomes. Through meditation the unconsciousness becomes more conscious. The term meditation has come to apply to a wide range of different practises. However, the ultimate goal of meditation, is to establish a connection with one's deep inner self.

Can everyone meditate? The truth is that meditating isn't a race or a massive mystery to master—simply it's returning to the breath over and over again.

Trigger Management Tools

What if thoughts make the individual sexually aroused? Meditation has the potential to stimulate the imagination. Simply take control of the thought and let it go, then return your attention to your breathing and repeat.

Meditation is commonly done by sitting silently and observing one's body or thoughts, though it can take numerous forms. Before carefully exhaling, some people concentrate on their breath and feel it swell inside their chest. Some people pay close attention to their bodily sensations, listening to their entire body and allowing each sensation to exist in its own right. Others simply sit and observe as fresh ideas enter and exit their heads.

The ability to be totally present in one's own life is the art of mindfulness. It's a gentle strategy for increasing mental awareness and gaining a truer, more in-depth understanding of oneself and one's environment. Mindfulness practises have been demonstrated in studies to positively alter the brain, enhancing physical and mental health and promoting general well-being. It can help reduce anxiety, increase self-awareness, and assist with triggers and coping with feelings that aren't based in reality. Individuals can use meditation and mindfulness practises to bring their thoughts into the present moment and focus on the moment. As a result, they aid in stress relief by promoting detachment from distressing experiences and triggers and attachment to here and now. According to Lao Tzu

> *'If you are depressed, you are living in the past. If you are anxious, you are living in the future. If you are at peace, you are living in the present.'*

Mindfulness, according to the restructuring reward theory, can reduce addictive behaviours by reversing the natural rewards associated with addiction pleasures.

Many mindfulness meditation techniques have been developed with the goal of revealing the middle way between attachment to pleasure and aversion to pain, thereby reducing addiction triggers and craving. This provides a sophisticated technique of releasing the individual from the push and pull of psychological and physiological dysregulation, which are at the core of addiction. The brain is the only organ that can be changed by practise and experience, much like a muscle can be altered via exercise. When a sex addict acts out, his or her brain is unconsciously moulded in ways that work against them and prevent them from being mindful. Meditation and other mindfulness approaches work in a similar way, allowing people to rewire their brains for more control, awareness, and enjoyment. Being aware and present can assist in learning to cope with reality as it is rather than how it is perceived.

Electroencephalography (EEG) research has shown that the top philosophers, thinkers, scientists, and inventors in the world use both hemispheres of the brain simultaneously. Mindfulness meditation helps to balance the brain's two hemispheres, forcing them to work together. Scientists call this *'whole brain synchronisation,'* because it causes extremely beneficial changes in hemispheric blood flow and chemistry. What does this imply for you personally? There are infinite benefits that will stack up over time. Your mind will become more alert, focused, profound, and active while remaining calm. Integrating both hemispheres of your brain and allowing them to work in sync will improve your overall mental health. Learning ability, consciousness, and executive function will all improve as a result of this. Furthermore, you'll discover that you have an endless supply of smart ideas, considerably less anger, resentment, despair, and compulsive behaviours. As a result, you'll be happier, more positive, and more connected with the rest of the world and creation.

To practise mindfulness meditation, one must pay attention to the breath as it inhales and exhales, as well as observe when the mind wanders away. Returning to the breath strengthens the muscles of attention and mindfulness. When we focus on our breath, we are learning how to intentionally return to and remain in the present moment and how to ground ourselves in the here and now without judgement. The mind of a sex addict is full of chatter and very hectic. Mindfulness can be used to take a break from a hectic day, or mind. A mindful check-in is, at its most basic level, about directing the attention on some essential questions. Mindfulness appears to be a simple concept—it requires patience to practise. Indeed, Sharon Salzberg, a well-known meditation teacher, recalls how her first meditation experience taught her how easily the mind gets distracted by other things.

> *'I thought, okay, what will it be, like, 800 breaths before my mind starts to wander? And to my absolute amazement, it was one breath, and I'd be gone,' says Salzberg (2021).*

Meditating for 12 minutes five times a week can improve serenity and attention capacity. Meditation has a number of other advantages:

- Reduced cortisol levels in the blood
- Increased feelings of well-being
- Reduced stress and depression
- Deeper relaxation
- Enhanced memory
- Lower stress
- Improve focus

A Simple example of how to Mindful Meditate

Start with 5-10 minutes of meditation practise. The best time to do it is first thing in the morning, before consuming any caffeine. Aim to meditate on a regular basis and for extended periods of time.

For best results, meditate for at least twenty minutes a couple of times per week. Meditation will become more comfortable, and the daily five minute sessions will be more successful.

To enhance your meditation practise, install a meditation app and listen to relaxing music.

1) Sit in a comfortable upright position.
   You might fall asleep if you're lying down particularly if your body is tired or sleep deprived. Instead, sit in a supportive chair with an upright back, or get a cushion or a yoga mat and sit on it.
2) Take some deep breaths in and out. Begin by inhaling and exhaling slowly, counting to five on each exhale and inhale. Inhale, then exhale gently through your nose, allowing your shoulders to relax. Repeat.
3) Gently close your eyes to help you concentrate. When your eyes are open, it's easy to give your mind a reason to stray.
4) Begin by scanning your entire body for any sensations or tension. It's a chance to check in with your body, which is a great approach to bring yourself into the present moment. Work your way up to the top of your head, starting with your feet, calves, hips, and so on and work your way up to the top of your head. If you notice any tension in your body, send breath in the direction of that body part and allow it to relax.

5) Be aware of your thoughts and notice them without judging them. Consider yourself an observer, and each thought is a cloud in the sky or a leaf in a flowing stream. Observe what thoughts are present and allow each one to emerge and drift away without judgement or attachment.
6) When your mind wanders, focus on your breath. Your attention will inevitably leave the breath and stray to other things. Simply return your focus to the breath when you notice your mind has wandered. The most important tool for staying grounded, connected, and focused in the moment is your breath. When you concentrate on breathing, your heart rate slows and your mind becomes quiet.
7) Gently open your eyes and with kindness return to the space when you're ready. When you're ready, gently lift your gaze. Take the time to listen to the sounds around you. Observe and pay attention to how your body is feeling right now, as well as your thoughts and feelings.

Questions About Meditation and Mindfulness

⁇ How and why do you think you'll be able to find time to meditate?

_____

_____

_____

_____

⑦ Do you utilise meditation apps and audio guides? Or try without? What did you find to be the most effective?

_____

_____

_____

_____

⑦ How often do you examine a mental to-do list while meditating? (for example, what do you have to do)?

_____

_____

_____

_____

⑦ How often do you feel peaceful and tranquil during meditation?

_____

_____

_____

_____

Trigger Management Tools

⑦ How often do you get irritated by unwanted recollections while meditating?

_____

_____

_____

_____

⑦ How often do you feel particularly aware of difficulty sustaining your attention on your breathing while meditating (for example, due to mind wandering).

_____

_____

_____

_____

⑦ During meditation, how often do you become aware of your own body?

_____

_____

_____

⑦ How often do you feel engaged in and aware of your breathing process during meditation?

___

⑦ When your mind wanders during meditation, what should you do?

___

⑦ What does falling asleep during meditation indicate?

___

Trigger Management Tools

⑦ For the next 30 days, how often and for how long do you plan to mediate?

___

⑦ What is going on inside of you and how do you feel right now?

___

⑦ How can you pause and stay present in your experience right now?

___

⑦ Are you aware of your own particular triggers and how they relate to your automatic responses?

_____

_____

_____

_____

⑦ Do you take a moment to pause, pay attention, and notice before responding, or do you react automatically to individuals or your surroundings?

_____

_____

_____

_____

⑦ What have been the consequences of your past heightened mindless reactivity?

_____

_____

_____

Trigger Management Tools

⁇ The emotional consequences?

_____

_____

_____

_____

⁇ The physical consequences?

_____

_____

_____

_____

⁇ The social consequences?

_____

_____

_____

_____

⓪ The spiritual consequences?

_____
_____
_____
_____

⓪ The sexual consequences?

_____
_____
_____
_____

⓪ What changes do you need to make to pause and function more mindfully?

_____
_____
_____
_____

CHAPTER 4

Acting in and Acting out
Identify Your Acting in Behaviours

Behaviours or attitudes that are meant to create distance and occur right before acting out are referred to as 'acting in.' In addicts, stress and tension build up over time, resulting in a loss of control in their addictive behaviours. So, how did that build-up of stress happen? It is the outcome of acting in a certain way. Acting in is simply a mindset that states, 'I can manage this on my own'.

Some of the acting in behaviours can take the form of:
- Defensiveness- taking things personally rather than accepting responsibility for one's actions and putting in the effort necessary to achieve. A person who is continuously on the defensive in all parts of their lives may be insecure or suffering from internal problems.
- Escape to fantasy - entertaining lustful thoughts and fantasies.
- Compulsive working out.
- Self-victimization, perceiving oneself as a victim.
- Suppressing negative emotions.
- Entitlement- communicates that the receiver has a 'right' to the rewards.
- Distracting self with too much work.
- Isolation and distancing from others.
- Delusions- are faulty beliefs that are unfounded in reality. 'I have the power to stop at any time,' or 'recovery/ therapy is essentially a sort of punishment,' are examples of delusions.
- Avoidance - the act of retreating from interpersonal relationships as a protective strategy against rejection, accountability, criticism, or exposure.
- Anger outburst- quitting sex addiction is challenging, and new experiences without the old coping mechanisms are often unpleasant and irritating. When withdrawing from addiction, anxiety, and frustration are frequent and commonly lead to anger.
- Catastrophizing - is the practise of immediately anticipating the 'worst case scenario' and labelling minor or moderate problems or challenges as catastrophic disasters.
- Controlling behaviours or attitudes - someone who is 'controlling' seeks to control situations to an unhealthy degree or tries to control other people to meet their own demands even at the expense of others. These people can

deceive their victims, insult, humiliate, or shame them in order to build a dependency. Alternatively, they can create settings in which the victim explodes in order for the controller to justify their overbearing behaviour.
- Dissociation - or a lack of presence is a psychology term that refers to a mental disconnection from reality.
- Risky behaviours - are those that have previously set the stage for compulsive sexual behaviour. For example, allowing wandering eyes to objectify, travelling through a given area of town, surfing the web, dressing up in a certain way, or engaging in flirtatious conversations. These actions are deliberate decisions that make it increasingly difficult to say 'No!' to sexually compulsive behaviours over time.

PRACTICAL RECOVERY TOOLS

The good news is that the addict who has started acting in still has hope. All of the things that the addict dislikes when they first begin acting in are likely to be suitable:

- Identifying and acknowledging the behaviours is the first step
- reaching out
- contacting a reliable friend

- meditating
- journaling
- attending a support group
- seeing an addiction therapist.

Acting in Questions

⁇ How many of the above acting ins have you identified that apply to you?

_____

_____

_____

_____

⁇ Have you identified other acting ins not listed above? What are they?

_____

_____

_____

_____

Identify Your Acting in Behaviours

⑦ Do you have unsupervised access to any computer, extra cash, a phone with internet access, or other such items?

___

⑦ Do you stay up late when this is a trigger for you?

___

⑦ Are you still around people that trigger you to act out or watch pornography, such as relatives, co-workers, authority figures, drinking buddies, drug dealers, or others?

___

⑦ Are you driving through locations where you used to act out?

_____

_____

_____

_____

⑦ Do you still subscribe to online movie services or publications that include triggering content?

_____

_____

_____

_____

⑦ Are you drinking when this is either a triggering or a pre-acting out ritual for you?

_____

_____

_____

_____

Identify Your Acting in Behaviours

⓻ What are your primary acting in behaviours?

_____

_____

_____

_____

⓻ When do you notice these behaviours?

_____

_____

_____

_____

⓻ What impact do acting ins have on your relationships, ability to function, and recovery?

_____

_____

_____

_____

⑦ What are the resources that you can use when these behaviours show up?

_____

_____

_____

_____

Acting in vs Acting out

Acting in, if left uncontrolled, lays the foundation for subsequent acting out behaviours.

Acting out refers to when a person decides to do something they want even if they know it is inappropriate. Because they are aware that what they are doing is inappropriate, they will frequently try to conceal it. Acting out is the start of the release phase of the sex addiction cycle when the addict is on the verge of slipping or relapsing.

Here are a few examples of acting out:

- Watching pornography
- Masturbating
- Phone sex
- Anonymous sex
- Voyeurism
- Exhibitionism

Denial and Acting Out

Addicts, particularly sex addicts, use denial as a powerful coping mechanism to avoid facing the truth. It means that the person can continue to engage in the behaviours even if it is manifestly harmful to their lives and the lives of others. Denial is a mental state in which the person denies or misrepresent what is actually going on. Denial is frequently utilised by addicts to shield their ego when they act out. It enables them to maintain the belief that their actions are rational and justifiable. The individual will believe that what they are doing is reasonable or normal, and anyone who tries to intervene will be suspected of having malicious reasons. Denial feeds the sex addiction and has serious consequences ranging from health problems to strained relationships.

A person in denial may engage in a variety of behaviours, including:

- Minimizing- saying things like 'I am not addicted,' 'It's not that bad,' or 'other people do a lot more than I do.'
- Rationalizing- addicts will justify their behaviour by claiming that they are stressed and need a little help getting through, that they have earned a reward for their hard work or are simply entitled. Another example is 'pornography and compulsive sexual activities are okay because everyone is doing them'.
- Self-Deception- is a powerful denial strategy in which a person tells himself that things aren't as bad or as serious as they appear to be, or their actions do not hurt others.
- Blaming others.
- Manipulating behaviours.
- Compliance the individual appears to go along with what is demanded of them in this pattern but displays no genuine change.

PRACTICAL RECOVERY TOOLS

Sadly, getting through denial is a difficult task. Addicts frequently must 'hit rock bottom' before they can confront the realities of their issues. This is a state that can last anywhere from a few days to a few weeks for some people. Others may have to wait months or even years. Another factor to think about is the degree to which addicts feel powerless in life. They may be more honest with themselves about how they acknowledge that they will never be able to manage everything and everyone in their life. Addict" need for denial and other self-destructive addictive behaviours will diminish if they can instead become aware of what they can truly control and how they can do so. Consequently, they will be able to start learning how to live more authentically.

- **Self-awareness**—being aware of one's feelings and behaviours is crucial to addiction recovery and long-term sobriety.
- **Admission** to have an addiction- the first and most important step in sex addiction recovery is admitting that there is a problem and dependency with lust and sex.
  - Sex addiction **therapy.**
  - **Reaching out** for help.
  - **Journaling**- processing emotions and experiences.

Identify Your Acting in Behaviours

- **Consequences-** negative consequences, such as the depletion of a bank account, end of a relationship or loss of a job due to addiction can be a major wake-up call.
- **Identify** any irrational beliefs you have about your situation.
- **Education-** many people are unaware that they have an addiction, but by reading educational materials about various addictions, they may be able to spot certain behaviours in themselves.
- **Learning** to become emotionally vulnerable with safe people.
- Being **receptive** when others point out one's blind spots.

Denial Questions

⁇ What kinds of denial-related behaviours are you using?

_____

_____

_____

_____

_____

⁇ Which denial pattern is your primary one?

_____

_____

_____

_____

⁇ What effect does denial have on your relationships and your recovery?

_____

_____

_____

_____

⁇ Has a history of denial played a role in your past relapse? How?

_____

_____

_____

_____

Identify Your Acting in Behaviours

⑦ Do you place blame on others for your addiction, (i.e., your parents, partner, children, or others)?

_____

_____

_____

_____

⑦ Do you experience any negative effects as a result of your denial, both for yourself and others? How?

_____

_____

_____

_____

⑦ Is your denial fear based? How?

_____

_____

_____

_____

(?) Do you receive or reject feedback?

___

___

___

___

(?) What resources do you have to address your denial?

___

___

___

___

CHAPTER 5

Positive Self-regulation

Positive self-regulation helps to reset physiological systems and re-establish equilibrium after experiencing a stressor. Any behaviour that an individual performs to manage their emotional state on their own is referred to as self-soothing or self-regulation. These behaviours are frequently formed in the early years of life, are habitual in character and are frequently regarded as calming or reassuring by the individual. Reaching for an alcoholic drink, searching the internet for sexual images, masturbating, compulsive gaming or gambling, or simply eating something unhealthy are all common and unhealthy self-soothing behaviours that cause further distress in the long run.

According to studies, positive and recurring self-regulation involves not only the start but also the maintenance of behavioural change, as well as the prevention of undesirable behaviours and healthy responses to situational demands. Inadequate self-regulation has been linked to poor self-control and increased impulsivity. This is due to increased limbic system (the unconscious part of the brain) activity and decreased prefrontal cortex activity (the conscious part of the brain). Addictions like substance or sex addiction have also been shown to undermine self-regulation by transferring activity from the prefrontal cortex to the limbic system. As a result, practising conscious and daily self-regulation during sex addiction recovery is critical and absolutely necessary. This will ensure that detrimental patterns of negative self-soothing behaviours are reversed while also increasing the likelihood of surrendering. Surrendering and letting go is only possible when a person learns to positively self-sooth or self-regulate their emotions.

Self-regulation is the physical and psychological control of self without the use of external control. Inability and lack of self-regulation, as well as maladaptive self-sooting / self-regulating behaviours, are the root causes of sex addiction. Emotional self-regulation, or the ability to keep one's emotions under control, is a critical aspect of sex addiction recovery and refers to the ability to govern impulsive and compulsive behaviours that could lead to relapse. Self-regulation leads to behavioural-regulation and consciousness. Behavioural control is defined as the ability to operate in one's best long-term interests while staying faithful to one's actual core values. Self-regulation, is a constantly active process in which you need to:

- Keep track of your own actions, and the effects and consequences of them on yourself and others.
- Assess your actions in light of your own personal values as well as broader, more contextual principles.
- Pay attention to your own activities, reflect on them, and respond to them, and examine what you believe and how you feel about them.

PRACTICAL RECOVERY TOOLS

Some of the many types of healthy self-soothing practises to explore is 5 senses or sensory soothing, opposite actions and fact checking.

Five senses or sensory soothing- is a simple but very effective approach to achieve self-regulation. This can be done using the five senses (*sight, hearing, taste, smell*, and *touch*). All you have to do is be present, focus on your senses, and let yourself be completely absorbed in the sensory experience. This is how it's done:

Step 1-Take 5 deep breaths in and out.
Step 2- Name 4 items you see.
Step 3-Name 3 objects you can touch.
Step 4-Name 2 things you hear.
Step 5-Name 1 thing you can smell.

Opposite action and check the facts
Thoughts and actions/behaviours are intricately linked, cannot be separated, and form a feedback loop in which each actively stimulates the other. When you have a thought, you experience a specific emotion, which is usually followed by a specific behaviour depending on that emotion. To put it

another way, T (thoughts) influence E (emotions), which influences A (actions/behaviours) **Figure 2.**

Figure 2 illustrates how thoughts impact emotions and emotions impact actions.

For example, you may believe someone has disrespected you (thought), become enraged (feeling), and fight (behaviour) with them, or the thought may make you sad, causing you to withdraw yourself from others. Ultimately, your body causes you to react to your thoughts and emotions in a certain way. Another concrete example of sex addiction is when you entertain lustful thoughts then you experience uncontrollable emotions and cravings, which lead to you acting out behaviours.

> *'Your beliefs become your thoughts, Your thoughts become your words, Your words become your actions, Your actions become your habits, Your habits become your values, Your values become your destiny'.*
> Mahatma Gandhi

Engaging in opposite actions means challenging the initial negative or unpleasant thought. Assess the truthfulness of that thought. Is it based on feelings or facts? Having a thought does not always imply that it is real. To help minimise the strength of these intense emotions, check the facts in the moment. Choose to examine the facts to assist you to change your emotional response and make healthier decisions as a result of unpleasant

Positive Self-regulation

emotions. You can adjust your response to a level suitable for the situation or respond with a more appropriate attitude by using check the facts and doing the opposite actions.

Ask yourself:
- Do the facts justify the intensity of my emotional responses?
- What can I do that is the total opposite of my usual reaction?
  - For example, instead of yelling when you're angry, consider speaking quietly and kindly.

Self-soothing or self-regulation examples

1) Focus on your breathing.
2) Change your environment.
3) Stretch and move your body.
4) Journaling.
5) Engage in a creative activity such as painting, dancing or playing an instrument.
6) Play a game of chess.
7) Take a shower or bath.
8) Tranquil imagery. Such as a burning candle, soft lighting, photographs of loved ones, affirmations etc.
9) Relaxing music.
10) Practice self-love and self-compassion by speaking kindly and lovingly to yourself out loud.
11) Mindful walking.
12) Meditation.
13) Practice 5 senses or sensory soothing.

How to self-regulate during a triggering event

1-Take a breath, pay attention, notice and identify what is going on, both cognitively and emotionally.

2-Select appropriate coping strategies (e.g., sitting in emotions, praying, journaling, connecting with others, therapy, and so on).

3- Engage your healthy coping skills.

When you utilise positive self-soothing techniques your brain can shift control away from the limbic system towards the prefrontal cortex for more executive decision-making. Consequently, your brain will begin to rewire itself and become accustomed to the new pattern of self-soothing and self-control as you repeatedly employ the same healthy self-regulating methods.

In contrast, if you continue to give in and engage in unhealthy self-soothing behaviours, you will just reinforce your brains previous programming and enhance the responsiveness of the limbic system.

Self-Soothing and Self-Regulation Questions:

⑦ What do you know about your old self-soothing strategies that aren't working?

_____

_____

_____

Positive Self-regulation

_____

_____

_____

⟨?⟩ What do you need to do in order to switch to healthy self-soothing and self-regulating techniques?

_____

_____

_____

_____

⟨?⟩ Is it necessary to change your environment? Why?

_____

_____

_____

_____

⍰ What will you do differently the next time a trigger occurs to help with self-regulation?

_____

_____

_____

_____

⍰ What is the most efficient strategy to prepare for the next trigger?

_____

_____

_____

_____

⍰ Do you have a habit of failing to see the consequences of your actions until it is too late? What, in your opinion, is the reason?

_____

_____

_____

_____

Positive Self-regulation

⑦ Are you confident that you can practice self-regulation? Explain.

_____

_____

_____

_____

⑦ Do you get thrown off track by minor issues or distractions? Explain.

_____

_____

_____

_____

⑦ What can you do to increase your emotional tolerance for life's challenges?

_____

_____

_____

_____

⑦ What are the self-regulation approaches that you have chosen to use? Why?

_____

_____

_____

_____

_____

⑦ How will self-regulation assist you in your ongoing sobriety?

_____

_____

_____

_____

_____

_____

Opposite Actions and Fact Checking Questions:

⑦ Where do your negative feelings usually originate from?

_____

_____

_____

_____

_____

⑦ What kind of thoughts do you have before you experience the unpleasant emotion(s)?

_____

_____

_____

_____

_____

_____

⁇ Describe the facts that you noticed when you are experiencing negative feelings or triggers?

_____

_____

_____

_____

⁇ What are your views, assumptions, and interpretations of the triggers?

_____

_____

_____

_____

⁇ What unpleasant feeling do you want to change?

_____

_____

_____

_____

Positive Self-regulation

⓶ With your feelings founded on facts, how would you deal with a dire situation?

___

___

___

___

___

___

⓶ What are some actions you can take the next time you're triggered and have cravings?

___

___

___

___

___

___

CHAPTER 6

Breaking Denial And De-Shaming Oneself With Honest Self-Disclosure

A disclosure is a prepared admission of previous wrongdoings, is planned and never done spontaneously. A disclosure occurs when an addict tells a trusted same-gender friend, family member, or spouse about their sexually acting out behaviours.

This approach, is highly sensitive and should be prepared with the help of a sex addict therapist. A disclosure is a therapeutic event that should be carried out under the supervision of a sex addiction therapist. The therapist walks the addict through the disclosure process and encourages them to prepare. The therapist also provides guidance on what and how much information to disclose. Failure to take therapeutic actions prior to a complete disclosure can result in trauma experiences for themselves and others.

Without assisted preparation, many sex addicts relapse shortly before or after making a disclosure to a same gender support person.

A disclosure can be used for a variety of objectives. For the addicts, a therapeutic prepared disclosure serves to de-shame them and assist them in recognising and breaking their own denial patterns. Additionally, disclosure is usually done to help the spouse understand the level of the addicts' powerlessness and unmanageability, with the goal of saving the relationship.

PRACTICAL RECOVERY TOOLS

Advantages of timely, planned, structured, and supervised disclosure to the sex addict:

- Gaining a better understanding of the consequences of addictive behaviours.
- Decreasing denial of and enslavement to character flaws, as well as addiction.

Breaking Denial And De-Shaming Oneself With Honest Self-Disclosure

- Self-trust and entrusting the disclosure to trustworthy persons can help to de-shame and promote self-esteem.

Maintain your **SAFETY** during the disclosure preparation process and afterwards through working with a sex addiction qualified therapist.

Support and Soothe yourself with selfcare.
Affirm and appreciate your recovery goals.
Focus on future hopes, relapse prevention and recovery plan.
Engage encouraging people around you.
Trust the truth to set you free.
Yearn for your long-term sobriety.

Self-Disclosure Questions

Sex addiction includes but is not limited to pornography viewing, masturbation, emotional, physical and online infidelity, non-genital sexual touch, sexting, webcamming, phone chats, prostitutes, escorts, strip clubs and bars, massage parlours, random sexual encounters, one night stands, bestiality, sexual fantasies and preoccupations

⑦ What were the compulsive sexual activities you engaged in?

_____

_____

_____

_____

? When it comes to disclosure, what are your biggest hopes and fears?

___

? Have you ever been infected with a sexually transmitted disease (STD)?

___

Breaking Denial And De-Shaming Oneself With Honest Self-Disclosure

⁇ Give a time frame for each sexual behaviour stated above. When it began and when it ended?

___

___

___

___

___

⁇ What was the frequency and duration of each of the above behaviours?

___

___

___

___

___

___

⑦ Give the financial cost of each of the behaviours described above, including lost wages, time spent, missed work, and so on?

_____

_____

_____

_____

_____

⑦ What has sex addiction cost you in terms of your relationship/ marriage, children, family, friends, and so on?

_____

_____

_____

_____

_____

Breaking Denial And De-Shaming Oneself With Honest Self-Disclosure

⑦ What has been the emotional, physical, sexual, and spiritual costs of your sex addiction?

_____

_____

_____

_____

⑦ What character defects have played a role in your sex addiction?

_____

_____

_____

_____

⑦ How did your sex addiction progress?

_____

_____

_____

_____

CHAPTER 7

Self-Care Before and After Disclosure

Anything that refuels and recharges the mind, body, and spirit is considered self-care. Self-care might range from maintaining personal cleanliness and physical health to engaging in activities that enhance mental and spiritual well-being.

Sobriety is only one aspect of sex addiction recovery. Sex addiction has significant impacts on the mind, body, and spirit. Addiction recovery aims to restore and maintain health in all areas of one's life. Self-care is about making the transition to a new, healthier way of life.

Addicts in recovery regularly express their exhaustion, claiming that it is difficult for them to perform all of their recovery tasks. They frequently have a history of bad time management, laziness, procrastination, poor performance, family arguments, and approaching financial disasters. Unfortunately, the recovering addicts find it difficult to accept that the majority of the drama in their life is self-inflicted, avoidable, and that it is the result of poor self-care.

Changes in your lifestyle have a direct impact on your mental and physical health. Emotional, physical, mental, social and spiritual self-care allow addicts to create a plan that ensures they are at their best during their recovery. Moreover, it is the conscious attention dedicated to your own well-being on all levels. In sex addiction recovery, self-care is a practise, not just a perception, it is a must and not a maybe.

PRACTICAL RECOVERY TOOLS

Emotional Self-care Includes:

- Sex Addiction therapy by a specialist.
- Journaling.
- Using positive self-affirmations.
- Meditation.
- Practising gratitude, both verbally and in writing.

Physical Self-Care Includes:

- Exercising (e.g., walking, running, swimming, biking, going to the gym, etc.).
- Taking a bath that is both restful and rejuvenating.
- Dancing to your favourite tunes.
- Home yoga and stretching.
- Power napping (a brief period of sleep done during the day to restore mental ability).
- Getting to bed at a reasonable hour.
- Regularly eating nutritious meals.
- Drinking enough water on a daily basis.
- Eating some chocolate or ice cream.

Mental Self-Care Includes:

- Trying out a new hobby or activity.
- Visiting a museum or an art gallery.
- Listening to informative podcasts or reading books.
- Playing an instrument or learning a new one.
- When possible, taking mental health breaks.
- Engaging in a fun but pro-sobriety activity.
- Playing chess.

According to research, chess has shown to aid with the symptoms or severity of a range of illnesses, such as dementia, ADHD, and panic attacks. Playing this tough game can help people achieve a condition of receptivity and improve the efficacy of their therapy sessions. Finally, chess offers various cognitive benefits, including the ability to boost:

- Intelligence
- empathy memory
- abilities in planning and problem-solving
- creative capabilities.

Why Social Self-Care?

As a fundamental aspect of our design, being a human requires us to connect and relate to others. Individual's social well-being is also ensured when their need for healthy connections is satisfied. Nevertheless, in the context of addiction recovery, self-care entails taking into account holistic aspects of a human being, especially the social aspects.

PRACTICAL RECOVERY TOOLS

Social Self-Care Includes:

- Constructing a socially supportive system by forming a five-person circle.

This is a group of at least 5 people who are pro-sobriety and with whom a person chooses to socialise and keep in touch. When and if necessary, the group assists and encourages the individual, as well as collaborates with them on problem solving.

- Initiating connections with friends and family members by phone or in person.
- Attending sobriety meetings.
- Attending therapy.
- Making an effort to socialise with pro-sobriety friends.
- Taking the significant other out on a date.
- Appreciating someone via writing a letter or sending a card.
- Playing and spending time with a pet.
- More listening and less talking.
- Doing random acts of kindness.

Why Spiritual Self-Care?

Spiritual self-care is defined as any ritual or activity that we engage in to strengthen our connection to our true self or higher self. The true-self, is who one genuinely is as an individual, separate from and unaffected by the ego or fear. It is the pure expression of a person's true good essence before any conditioning or restricting beliefs transpired. Spiritual self-care includes activities that aid in the development of a sense of connectedness to a higher power or God and a sense of purpose in life. Because it is just as vital to nourish and awaken the body with food as it is to nourish and awaken the soul with spirit, spiritual self-care allows for spiritual awakening to occur.

Spiritual awakening is a subjective experience in which one's ego transcends beyond their usual, finite sense of self to include a larger, infinite sense of truth or reality. In this space the consciousness connects and integrates with itself, allowing the spirit's wiser inner voice to be heard and received authentically and humbly.

PRACTICAL RECOVERY TOOLS

Spiritual Self-Care Includes:

- Praying.
- Reciting certain memorised prayers throughout the day.
- Nature-based activities.
- Engaging in spiritual/religious communities and practise.
- Doing home based yoga.
- Volunteering and community service.
- Mindfulness practice.
- Meditation.
- Reading and writing spiritual materials.
- Practicing gratitude.
- Practicing silence. According to a 2013 study of brain anatomy and function, two hours of silence can result in the formation of new brain cells in the part of our brains associated with learning and memory.

Self-Care Questions:

⑦ What does self-care mean to you?

_____

_____

_____

_____

⑦ What self-care rituals have you chosen for yourself?

_____

_____

_____

_____

⑦ Are you starting to feel drained?

_____

_____

_____

_____

Self-Care Before and After Disclosure

⑦ Are you being kind and good to yourself?

_____

_____

_____

_____

⑦ Do you make time for yourself, or do you get caught up in your daily activities?

_____

_____

_____

_____

⑦ How can you practise self-care so that your loved ones feel closer to you?

_____

_____

_____

_____

⑦ What are the potential benefits of your self-care to others?

_____

_____

_____

_____

⑦ How do you practice self-care without negatively impacting someone else?

_____

_____

_____

_____

⑦ What are some simple self-care routines you could do every day that would just take a few minutes?

_____

_____

_____

_____

Self-Care Before and After Disclosure

⁇ What new activities or hobbies (self-care) do you want to start?

_____

_____

_____

_____

⁇ Are your chosen self-care practices aligned with your sobriety?

_____

_____

_____

_____

⁇ Are you initiating social connections?

_____

_____

_____

_____

? Who are your nominated circle of five?

_____

_____

_____

? How are you practicing listening more and talking less?

_____

_____

_____

? How are you practicing intentional wholesome silence?

_____

_____

_____

_____

CHAPTER 8

Phases of Sex Addiction Recovery

The Five phases of change, also known as the trans-theoretical model, was developed in 1983 to assist smokers in quitting. It was later improved and put to clinical usage for a number of behaviours, including addiction recovery. These phases in the context of sex addiction recovery are often not sequential, or for a fixed period of time. Each phase of recovery comes with its own set of relapse risks.

Precontemplation phase- the addict has not yet acknowledged or admitted that there are problem behaviours that needs to be changed. Addicts defend their addictive behaviours and disregard them as a problem throughout this stage of addiction. Defensiveness, constant justification, and an evident lack of insight into their behaviours characterise this phase. When addicts are in the precontemplation phase, they are generally uninterested in learning about the negative consequences of their addiction or receiving advice on how to stop. Instead, they often get defensive if others try to urge them to seek help. Denial plays a huge role in this phase. In precontemplation, the majority of people fear they will never recover. The truth is that sex addiction can be overcome.

Contemplation- the addict is acknowledging that there is a problem but not yet ready or certain of wanting to make a change. Although addicts at this stage are capable of considering the idea of change, they are often conflicted and ambivalent. At this point, addicts are weighing the advantages and disadvantages of stopping or modifying their habits. Although addicts consider the negative aspects of their sex addiction as well as the benefits of quitting they may be sceptical that the long-term gains will exceed the short-term difficulties. The contemplation phase could take as little as a few weeks or as long as a lifetime to complete. In fact, some people think about ending their addiction over and over again, and they may never get past this stage. These individuals become the fatalities of their addiction.

Preparation and Determination- the addict is getting ready to change. Addicts have made a commitment to change at this point. People are now taking small steps towards understanding their addiction and quitting, much like they would during a research period. They are attempting to determine what they will need to do in order to change their habits, which may include reading books like this. Addicts are proactively looking for therapy, resources, and strategies to aid them in their recovery. If people skip this stage and go straight from contemplation to action phase, they will fail miserably because they haven't done enough investigation or acknowledged the true nature of their sex addiction. As a result, the significant transformative lifestyle change that is required to stay sober may shock individuals and impede their recovery.

Action- the addict is actively participating in recovery work and changing behaviours. This is the phase where addicts believe they have the potential to change and are actively engaged in changing their addictive behaviours through a number of strategies. This is the shortest of all the phases, usually lasting around six-twelve months. Individuals are most at risk of relapse since they are making overt efforts to cease or adjust their behaviours. Addicts evaluate their commitment to oneself mentally and plan tactics for dealing with internal and external challenges that could lead to relapse. Addicts in this phase are more willing to accept help and are more inclined to seek support from others which is a very important element for ongoing recovery.

Maintenance- the addict is working on maintaining the behavioural changes. Maintaining sobriety entails skilfully avoiding any temptations to return to addictive behaviours. The goal of the maintenance phase is to keep the new status quo or the new normal in place. Recovering addicts often reflect on how far they have come at this time. Successful individuals in this phase are constantly reformulating their life principles and finding new ways to interact with life in order to avoid relapse.

They can also predict and plan for scenarios when a relapse can occur, they apply the given recovery tools, as well as create coping methods ahead of time. Individuals in maintenance never lose sight of the fact that the sobriety they are pursuing is meaningful and significant. As a result, they practise patience with themselves and recognise that creating new behaviours and modifying old ones takes time, but these new habits will eventually become second nature. The maintenance phase can be the most difficult since, after a certain amount of time has passed, the focus on achieving the goal may fade. Consequently, People may become complacent at this point, feeling that a small slip-up will have little impact. However, staying sober is always easier than resuming sobriety following a relapse.

Relapse- an addict is returning to older addictive behaviours and abandoning the new changes. Understanding that relapse occurs gradually is crucial to preventing relapse. It takes days, weeks, or even months, before a person begins to act out.

There are three stages of relapse, according to research:

- **Emotional Relapse**
  Individuals commonly do not anticipate acting out during emotional relapse. They are aware of their previous relapse and do not wish to repeat it. However, their miss managed feelings and behaviours are preparing them for a future relapse. Denial is a key aspect of emotional relapse because addicts aren't consciously thinking about relapsing at this point.

Signs of emotional relapse:
- Suppressing emotions.
- Isolation or creating distance.
- Not attending meetings.
- Attending meetings but not sharing.
- Focusing on other people or their problems, or how other people affect them.
- Unhealthy eating, working and sleeping habits.
- Poor self-care.

- **Mental Relapse**
    There is intense tension and war going on inside the addicts' mind during mental relapse. One Part wants to give in to urges and cravings, but another part doesn't. As individuals progress deeper into mental relapse, their cognitive resistance to relapse weakens, but their desire to escape or medicate increases. During a mental relapse, bargaining is an intense and common occurrence.

    During bargaining, individuals begin to imagine scenarios in which acting out might be justifiable. This is a classic example of people giving themselves permission to act out during holidays or work trips. Airports and all-inclusive resorts are known to be high-risk situations during the early stages of recovery.

    Another type of bargaining occurs when individuals begin to believe that they can relapse on a regular basis, perhaps once or twice a year. Switching one addictive behaviour or substance for another is also a type of bargaining. Clinical experience has shown that if a person is in mental relapse for a long time without the proper coping skills, they are more prone to physical relapse.

Signs of mental relapse:
- Increased cravings.
- Thinking about people, places, and things that have been linked to previous acting out behaviour.
- Minimizing the consequences of past behaviours or glorifying past acting out.
- Lying.

- Developing strategies to mitigate the effects of an imminent relapse.
- Looking for relapse ideas.
- Bargaining (mental negotiations).
- Making preparations for a relapse.

- **Physical Relapse**
  Finally, physical relapse occurs when a person begins to act out sexually. Some researchers distinguish between a lapse (the initial acting out behaviours) and a relapse (the follow up sexual behaviours and a return to uncontrolled activities). The recovering person's identification of the mistaken or unwelcome behaviours, as well as their re-commitment to recovery, is the important feature that distinguishes this behaviour as a lapse rather than a relapse.

  A plan to avoid repeating the same lapse is included in the re-commitment. A relapse, on the other hand, occurs when a person in recovery abandons their recovery for a lengthy period of time accompanied with a negative mindset such as 'What's the use in trying to stay sober anymore?' Or 'I can never stay sober so, why bother?'

CHAPTER 9

Causes of Relapse After a Period of Sobriety

1) The leading cause of relapse is stress. The most common cause of relapse is stress and many individuals who battle with sex addiction use their chosen sexual activities as maladaptive coping techniques. When people are anxious or stressed, their desire and cravings for addictive behaviours increase, especially if the behaviours have been the person's go-to coping techniques.
2) Individuals begin to focus less on self-care as their lives improve or taking on more obligations. In a sense, they are trying to get back to their old life (the old normal) without sex addiction. As a result, many stop engaging in

the healthy activities and change that contributed to their recovery.

3) Some people stop going to therapy or meetings because they don't feel like they're learning anything new. One of the advantages of continuing recovery work is that it serves as a reminder of the deceptive addiction's voice and how to recognise and respond to it.

4) Individuals in recovery believe they should go beyond the basics and find it almost unpleasant to discuss the basics of recovery. Some people are embarrassed to admit that they still have cravings or even deny that they have an addiction.

5) People who have been sober for a time grow arrogant and want to pick and choose which aspects of recovery work suits them. They are no longer willing to submit or surrender to the process of recovery.

6) Individuals begin to attend fewer meetings because they often desire to put their addiction behind them and forget they ever had one. Some people believe they have wasted a considerable amount of their lives due to addiction and do not want to spend the rest of their lives in recovery.

7) Socializing with people who have engaged in addictive behaviours with the addict, as well as the environments in which these behaviours happened.

8) Inability to manage negative or challenging emotions. Addicts frequently lack effective skills for enduring, regulating, and making sense of the negative emotions they face on a daily basis. As a result, compulsive sexual behaviours are utilised to provide temporary relief from those feelings, but this detrimental pattern of behaviour must be changed during the recovery process. It is normal and acceptable for everyone to have negative or challenging emotions; the goal is to cope with them in a wholesome manner.

Causes of Relapse After a Period of Sobriety

9) Refusing to make the necessary lifestyle changes for true recovery. Instead, reverting to an old, comfortable and familiar pattern of behaviours. Recovery is about more than just stopping and straying; it is about developing a new life that is safer and more enjoyable without resorting to acting out. When individuals dwell on the losses of the momentary pleasures that their addiction provided, they may feel they miss their previous lives when, in fact, sex addiction only provided pain and suffering. Instead, they need to concentrate on the gains of sobriety.

10) Relapse might be triggered by happy occasions such as birthdays and holidays. Individuals may feel in control and self-assured that, among other things, they can handle a little flirtation or indulge in lustful thoughts or acts.

11) Putting themselves in the midst of temptation is a guaranteed way for an addict to lose the ability to recognise when and how to stop. As a result, a casual glance at pornography or web browsing could quickly escalate into a sexual binge. Sex addicts are often surprised at how quickly their good intentions fade once they convince themselves that they can handle temptation rather than avoid it.

11) Complacency and lack of ongoing preparation for risky situations ahead of time after a period of sobriety. A significant component in prevention would be to always brainstorm ideas ahead of time and work with a therapist to develop a plan.

The relapse phase can sometimes be included in the process of recovery to recognise that an addict may have a few minor or major relapses before achieving maintenance. If the causes for the relapse are understood and handled, a relapse can be useful and employed in an ongoing active recovery plan with a relapse prevention plan. After repeated relapses, individuals may begin to understand what recovery from sex addiction means for them.

PRACTICAL RECOVERY TOOLS

- Therapy.
- Attending regular 12-step meetings.
- Reaching out to a same gender accountability person.
- Self-care.
- Identifying denial.
- Identifying high risk situations.
- Developing healthy exit strategies from risky situations.
- Developing a relapse prevention plan.
- Learning how to address negative emotions or stressors through journaling and meditation.

Recovery Phase Questions:

⑦ Identify whether you are recovering addict or a denied addict?

_____

_____

_____

_____

Causes of Relapse After a Period of Sobriety

⑦ Which phase of change or recovery are you in right now?

_____

_____

_____

_____

⑦ How do you know what phase of recovery you're in?

_____

_____

_____

_____

⑦ Who do you believe should make the necessary changes in this situation? Why?

_____

_____

_____

_____

⑦ Do you intend to stop your compulsive sexual behaviours?

_____

_____

_____

_____

⑦ How sure are you that you can break your sexual addiction? Why?

_____

_____

_____

_____

⑦ Do you admit you have an addiction?

_____

_____

_____

_____

_____

Causes of Relapse After a Period of Sobriety

⑦ What level of knowledge do you have about your sex addiction?

_____

_____

_____

_____

What level of knowledge do you have about recovery process?

_____

_____

_____

_____

⑦ Are there any behaviours that you need to change but you simply can't?

_____

_____

_____

_____

⑦ What is your plan to address the above challenges?

_____

_____

_____

_____

⑦ Do you have a plan to change your behaviours and recover from sex addiction?

_____

_____

_____

_____

⑦ Are you willing to make a comprehensive lifestyle change in order to maintain your sobriety?

_____

_____

_____

_____

Causes of Relapse After a Period of Sobriety

⑦ Give details about lifestyle changes you need to make in order to stay sober:

Personal changes

_____

_____

_____

_____

Occupational changes

_____

_____

_____

_____

Relational and social changes

_____

_____

_____

Sexual changes

_____

_____

_____

_____

Spiritual changes

_____

_____

_____

_____

(?) What is your action plan to maintain the changes?

_____

_____

_____

_____

Causes of Relapse After a Period of Sobriety

⑦ On a scale of 1 to 10, with 10 being the most confident and 1 being the least confident, how confident are you that you will maintain the changes necessary for your sobriety during the next week?

_____

_____

_____

_____

_____

⑦ Do you consider the changes permanent? Why?

_____

_____

_____

_____

_____

_____

⁇ Are you finding it difficult to maintain the changes you made to stay sober, or are they becoming more automatic?

_____

_____

_____

_____

⁇ Are you in a toxic relationship, facing financial difficulties, or dealing with other stressors?

_____

_____

_____

_____

⁇ When was your last relapse?

_____

_____

_____

_____

Causes of Relapse After a Period of Sobriety

⑦ Why do you think you relapsed?

_____

_____

_____

_____

⑦ Have you ever felt like relapsing after a previous relapse but didn't? What stopped you?

_____

_____

_____

_____

CHAPTER 10

Withdrawals

When recovering sex addicts stop acting out, they are often taken aback by the severity of their withdrawal symptoms. Almost every addict in early recovery struggles with the withdrawal process, which persists regardless of the addictive behaviour or substance they're trying to eliminate. Withdrawal is triggered by a reduction in dopamine production in the brain, which was previously inundated with dopamine from sexual acting out.

Symptoms aren't just physical; they can also affect the mind and how one perceives the environment (which can appear dark). When the brain's reward system and stress circuits become more dysregulated, withdrawal symptoms grow more severe. The more frequent and intense compulsive sexual behaviours are, the more severe the withdrawals become.

The good news is that withdrawal symptoms, no matter how severe, do pass. However, if the individuals' relapse or continue to act out before their brains return to normal sensitivity, they may find themselves in a Groundhog Day situation. Because all addictions share basic neurochemical and cellular changes that affect specific areas of the brain, withdrawal symptoms are similar.

According to recent study, withdrawal causes a sequence of neurochemical changes that result in lower levels of dopamine, opioids, endorphins, and GABA (an anti-anxiety neurotransmitter), as well as higher amounts of stress hormones. Furthermore, one week after stopping acting out, the reward centre creates new nerve cell branches, which correlate with increased cravings and urges.

Common withdrawal symptoms include:
- Insomnia or a lack of quality sleep.
- Isolation and a tendency to avoid socialising.
- Mood Swings, negative feelings, low enthusiasm and low mood.
- Inability to focus or concentrate.
- Depression, anxiety, stress, despair and other forms of sadness or fear.
- Flu, nausea, fever, muscle aches and pains, as well as stiffness in the joints, teeth, and genitals or other physical pain.
- Irritability, exhaustion, and weakness.
- Anger outbursts, defensiveness and negative attitude.
- Frustration, irritability, annoyance, short-temperedness and other forms of anger.
- Sexual urges, thoughts, dreams and flashbacks.

PRACTICAL RECOVERY TOOLS

- Therapy to resolve negative self-labelling and catastrophizing thinking.
- Repair relationships and make amends when possible.
- Tolerating to feel comfortable with being uncomfortable.
- Making self-care a component of recovery.
- Creating a healthy and balanced lifestyle.
- Engage in same gender groups and meetings.
- Developing healthy alternatives instead of acting out.
- Medication.

Some examples of what to expect when experiencing withdrawal symptoms:

Day 1-15 are commonly effortless and uncomplicated.

Day 16-30 are when urges are high, tiredness and sadness appear.

Day 30-60 urges are still there but with less intensity and changes in brain clarity are becoming more noticeable.

Day 60-80 are sometimes overshadowed with depression, anxiety while there is not many cravings or urges.

Day 80+ Smooth sailing, feeling overall good and in control.

However, the most crucial thing to remember about withdrawal is that it can persist (with lesser intensity) up to 2 years for some people.

Withdrawal Questions:

⑦ How long have you been engaging compulsive sexual acts?

_____

_____

_____

_____

Withdrawals

⁇ Have you engaged in sexual behaviour?

_____

_____

_____

_____

⁇ How often have you engaged in such activities?

_____

_____

_____

⁇ What kinds of sexual behaviours have you engaged in?

_____

_____

_____

_____

⑦ Have you ever experienced withdrawal symptoms after ceasing to act out?

_____
_____
_____
_____

⑦ How long after stopping acting out do you experienced withdrawal symptoms?

_____
_____
_____
_____

⑦ What withdrawal symptoms have you experienced?

_____
_____
_____
_____

Withdrawals

⁉ What resources can you use to reduce the withdrawals?

_____

_____

_____

_____

_____

CHAPTER 11

Non-negotiable Rules of Recovery

Change your beliefs and behaviours, and your brain will change, and as a result ultimately your life will change. You're choosing your addiction if you aren't changing your life. Every sex addict is on the lookout for a magical solution that doesn't exist. Recovery requires intentional, ongoing work and transformation. You have to create a new life in which it is easier to refrain from acting out, otherwise all of the factors that led to your sex addiction will catch up with you.

Practice brutal honesty with yourself and others. Self-deception and deceit of others are central to sex addiction. Lying to oneself and then lying to others constitutes self-deception. Before entering recovery, the majority of sex addicts have told so many lies that their own lies have become their reality. An emotional relapse occurs when sex addicts aren't entirely honest. Recovering sex addicts are advised to be completely honest with their primary support system before gradually expanding this to include additional trustworthy individuals. The primary support system includes family, therapists, health professionals, self-help groups and sponsors. Obviously, being honest all of the time may be difficult at first, but a helpful approach is to go back and redeem yourself if you have been dishonest with someone.

Seek help and support through therapy and self-help groups. The majority of addicts start their recovery on their own. Sex addicts often want to avoid shame, prove that they have control over their addiction (denial), or pretend that they are not as bad as others think (denial, self-deception and delusion). Intensive therapy and participation in a self-help group have been demonstrated to greatly reduce faulty beliefs and raise the likelihood of long-term recovery.

Don't pick and choose your recovery bits, and don't deviate from the rules. There are numerous examples of successful recovering sex addicts, but recovery only works as well as the honest work you put into it. If you keep looking for loopholes and exceptions, you will surely fail. Some people waste their time and money by attending therapy when they don't plan to do the required work or dismiss the professionals instructions. This is a clear indication that they are unwilling to give up lust, and the final effect is like driving a car with a flat tyre. A popular phrase goes, 'You can't be a little bit pregnant; you're either pregnant or you're not.' In other words, either you give up lust 100% or you're delusory enough to believe that this allergy will be under your control. When it comes to sex addiction recovery, you're either in or out, and if you're not fully immersed in recovery, you will BURN.

Non-negotiable Rules of Recovery

K.I.S.S- keep it simple and surrender. In the sex addiction community, surrendering is a widely misunderstood and misapplied concept. Struggling to stay sober is one of the indicators that someone is on the wrong path in their sex addiction recovery. Because it shows that the only thing keeping the person from acting out is an exhaustive effort of willpower, also known as white-knuckle sobriety. Grasping the true nature of the surrendering process is essential to achieving long-term sobriety. Surrendering is misunderstood by most sex addicts, who either overcomplicate it or just translate it as doing nothing, and thus miss out on its benefits. What does it mean to truly surrender in terms of recovery, and what is the connection between this and white knuckling?

The most prevalent cause of white-knuckle sobriety is ambivalence or a lack of surrender to the recovery process, which means the person is not entirely committed to giving up lust and committing to a new life.

'Surrender to Win' is how AA (Alcoholics Anonymous) refer to the process of surrender. Surrendering is a voluntary decision to stop fighting that is entirely within the individual's control. The level to which a person recovers is proportional to how much they surrender. Regaining control by giving up control is the concept of surrender during sex addiction recovery.

Surrender is being willing to live differently as well as being open-minded enough to see things from a new perspective. When you put your trust in the future, let the past go, and accept what is, you have surrendered. The person still believes that there is a way to entertain lust, which suggests that there is still a way to combat it. Sex addicts frequently silently hope that one day it will be safe to entertain lust or even act out (with some control and structure, certainly, another deceptive belief), but this is precisely what makes recovery difficult and inconsistent. One of the most difficult aspects of sex addiction recovery is that some people must suffer greatly, be completely broken, or reach rock bottom before realising they need to surrender. Genuine recovering sex addicts, on the other hand, surrender by committing 100% to a new life in which they give themselves 0% choice to entertain lust, relapse or act out.

Individuals become addicted as a result of their distorted thinking, and their attitude and mindset get them trapped in the cycle of addiction. To surrender in sex addiction recovery is to be willing to let go of old patterns of interacting with others and the environment. It takes humility to be willing to let go of beliefs and methods of thinking that negatively affect your life but surrendering demands it. If you continue to behave as if you believe that you already have all the answers, you have not surrendered.

When all else fails and addicts are left with no other options, they may consider recovery - surrendering to the realisation that they are powerless over their addiction and that they need the help of other people and resources.

Surrender vs giving up:
- Surrender, in contrast to giving up, which seems dismal and defeating, feels tranquil and is typically followed by a sense of great relief.
- Surrender has a rational or balanced sentiment while giving up is an unpleasant or overwhelming experience.
- Surrender is a deliberate and intentional cognitive decision but giving up is typically fuelled by strong emotional reactivities.
- Surrender embraces that the person may not have all of the necessary solutions and that it is critical to remain open to new options, whereas giving up blocks off potential prospects.

- Surrender is the conscious implementation of plans (i.e., recovery plans) as needed, whereas giving up is the diversion of non-recovery productive action plans or a shift in emphasis.
- Surrender entails a willingness to let go of one's ego. Ego is the aspect of human nature that is preoccupied with oneself, one's own desires, needs, and wants. There is no need to control the cravings and desires that addiction brings once the person surrenders and the ego is released. However, giving up, on the other hand, feels forced, unjustified, and egotistical.
- Surrender is a proactive, self-loving decision to secure one's individual freedom, and an act of personal responsibility that affirms one's self-worth. It is about intentionally and actively choosing to get off the insidious roller coaster of life. Giving up, on the other hand, is resignation, defeat, and abdication of responsibility.
- Surrender is a humble act that acknowledges the absolute imperfection of human nature. This humbling act can be perceived as humiliating for an addict who is both fearful of pain and carries pride. On the other hand, giving up activates fear, and the self-will strengthens its grasp and pushes even harder for the wants and desires. It also awakens pride, which keeps the idealised self-image and ego alive. Pride is formed from shame and rejection and presents itself as a sense of invulnerability or a drive to be correct or flawless. Its purpose is to deceive the heart into thinking it is guarding it from further pain.

Surrendering entails relinquishing control and letting go.
- Submitting to an entity and their authority or principles by letting go of fighting and getting rid of an old belief system and mindset that aren't useful.

- Processing and letting go of acquired junk from the past that keeps them trapped in a cycle of addictive behaviour.
- Addicts believe they can control their behaviour until they lose it again, and their inability to realise and accept that they cannot control their addiction once it has been ignited leads to even more intense instability and suffering. Surrendering implies that 'I realise that I am allergic to lust and that even a slight bite will kill me.' As a result, I will take whatever precautions are necessary to avoid getting myself into a risky situation.
- Surrendering implies that instead of resisting or fighting life, there is an acceptance of it. Acceptance does not imply approval. It signifies that a person has recognised reality and, rather than denying, rejecting, or fighting what is, they have acknowledged it and are taking positive steps to address it.
- Surrender means, accepting one's powerlessness over sex addiction is the first step towards reclaiming the power. As a result, pre-planning and avoiding temptations, as well as practising real-time trigger management, provides addicts with a tremendous sense of relief, as they won't have to fight their addiction but rather accept that they must address it properly before it gets out of hand.

People dedicate their activities, thoughts, relationships, aspirations, successes, and personal fulfilment to the addictive behaviours during active addiction.

Many people also feel that they are powerless, as addiction takes control of their brain and compels them to surrender to it. Individuals struggling with sex addiction frequently make commitments to work harder and resist temptations, but these promises are rarely accomplished. To grasp the complexity of addiction and the efficacy of the surrender process, we must first comprehend how the brain functions.

To solve problems, two areas of the brain collaborate. The way these two areas interact will determine one's wellbeing.

The neocortex and the pre-frontal cortex, is the higher-functioning area of the brain. The prefrontal cortex, often known as the executive function, is also practical, rational, and moral in that it makes sense of life's experiences. Consciousness is controlled by this area of the brain (which is weakened or malfunctions owing to compulsive sexual behaviours).

The limbic system is the brain's other unconscious and more primitive component and in charge of both survival and physiological functions (i.e., sexual urges).

Because morality and values do not exist in the limbic system, addictions can begin to form there. Although it is important to recognise that this part of the brain has a significant influence on behaviour, the limbic system alone cannot cause a person to behave in a specific manner. Sex addiction is a chemical imbalance in the brain.

One chemical of interest is dopamine, sometimes known as the pleasure chemical, which causes one to want and crave more of it. Compulsive sexual behaviours induce a spike in dopamine levels in the brain that can be ten times higher than normal. There is no simple mechanism for the brain to defend itself in this situation. By overwhelming the brain with dopamine and other chemicals at a rate and degree that is difficult to control, sex addiction creates a shortcut to the brain's normal function.

According to a recent article published by Harvard Health Publications.

> *'The brain registers all pleasures in the same way, whether they originate with a psychoactive drug, a monetary reward, a sexual encounter, or a satisfying meal. .. The likelihood that the use of a drug or participation in a rewarding activity will lead to addiction is directly linked to the speed with which is promotes dopamine release, the intensity of that release, and the reliability of that release. . . . In nature, rewards usually come only with time and effort'.(2022)*

The limbic system is built on the notion that addictive behaviours are necessary for survival. This is why relying solely on willpower to overcome an addiction will not be effective in the long run. To put it another way, one starts to fight the part of oneself that has linked survival needs to addictive behaviour. Surrender entails turning around and distancing from an enemy without fighting, but without becoming a victim of one's opponent.

> *Surrender, rather than willpower, may be the only notion that can cause beneficial changes in a person's sobriety owing to changes in brain chemistry.*

Surrender also signals the limbic system to relax and exit the survival mode, allowing the prefrontal cortex to activate and begin planning for thriving. Surrender must be approached as a deliberate act and a process of intentional conversion that must be repeated throughout the day. Refusing surrender is comparable to attempting to deceive destiny. It is possible to impose one's will on life and push one's way through it, but this ignores the critical virtues of perseverance, acceptance, hope, and humility that must be mastered. On certain levels, people may be successful in life if they skip over these virtues, but there is often a cost to the higher self in the form of shame, guilt, low self-esteem, and self-loathing. Worse, the opportunity for genuine self-development is squandered.

Failure to surrender to all aspects of recovery, including the **recovery process, personal, professional, sexual, relational/social**, and **spiritual** components, will result in failure to maintain sobriety in the context of sex addiction recovery.

Recovery surrender- rather than just stating you surrender or battling and white-knuckling to stay sober, surrendering to the recovery process entails following recovery steps, utilising multiple support systems, and deliberately employing what's in the therapeutic recovery tool box. Surrendering is an ongoing process and not a one off event. It means following therapeutic guidelines without resistance or modifications. Surrender in recovery refers to a person's purposeful, focused, and productive choices and active efforts in the direction of active recovery.

Surrendering is agreeing to the terms and conditions set forth by the therapist, sponsor, or support group to which you are surrendering. When a person claims to want to get sober but refuses to do the work that is required in their recovery, they have failed to surrender. Instead, they have decided to recover under their own conditions, which will never work. Surrender demands the recovering addict to become comfortable with being uncomfortable. Some of the required recovery activities may be excruciatingly unpleasant or constraining. Having accountability individuals to report to, installing filters or internet blockers, location trackers, journaling, and sitting in emotions and performing amendments are just a few examples. However, doing solely what feels comfortable will almost certainly result in lapses and relapses.

Recovery surrender recognises that you cannot conquer your addiction on your own, in denial, or with the same deceptive, manipulative, or controlling attitude you had before. Surrendering sometimes entails saying no and maintaining clear boundaries.

Sex addicts are notoriously poor at setting boundaries (lack of boundaries is a major part of sex addiction and its progress), surrendering to them early in the recovery process is important.

Personal surrender- learning from others with humility, surrendering to the sponsors, mentors, and 12-step fellowship without distorting or rejecting what has worked for others to suit your personal preferences, and without ego and without an 'I know best' attitude. In sobriety, personal surrender implies letting go of the impulse to control everything and everyone, as well as the desire to satisfy oneself at any costs.

Personal Surrender entails taking control of what is under one's power (such as one's own actions, reactions, and behaviours) while letting go of what is beyond one's control (such as other people's reactions, behaviours, and shortcomings). Surrendering involves actively working on improving and correcting one's character defects while allowing others to do so at their own pace.

Professional surrender- this process can provide serenity and satisfaction, as well as open the door to hope, transformation, and new professional prospects. It can also help to bring more positivity into one's professional life. Remaining in professional limbo (i.e., in a fight, flight, or freeze state) or quitting your current job for a new one are fears associated to work. When a person gives up in exasperation over work-related triggers or challenges, they may feel hopeless, trapped, empty, or ashamed of themselves.

Surrendering might entail leaving a job or even changing careers. Taking a break or reducing working hours can bring clarity into challenges and can be extremely beneficial in the early stages of recovery. Surrendering or even walking away from a physically or psychologically triggering job seems less like a defeat but a re-evaluation and enables individuals to better understand their own experiences and emotions.

Accepting your job situation, and trying to make the best of it is also an alternative. Professional surrender can necessitate staying and making peace with your existing employment. You make the decision to stop fighting the job and instead surrender and lean into it. This is true, when your profession is secure, doesn't jeopardise your sobriety, and your reasons for disliking it are based on your ego or other character defects.

Sexual surrender- this begins with an internal process in which you choose to defuse lustful thoughts rather than entertain them. While someone recovering from a sex addiction may occasionally view erotic images without acting out, this eventually leads to a pileup effect and derailment. At the end of the day, full-fledged sexual acting out starts with a lustful thought that wasn't surrendered but evolved in the mind.

Giving in to the compulsive sexual impulses entails admitting your powerlessness and severe allergy to lust. Individuals in recovery must understand that willpower alone is insufficient. Willpower is an addict's defence mechanism to always have a justification to act out in the future.

By surrendering to the power of sex addiction and learning to understand that addictive cravings will persist for the remainder of one's life, a person can avoid falling into the trap of temptation.

Sexual surrender implies that the addict's impulses are inevitable, but how he or she deals with them is what makes the difference. Preplanning, deleting triggering materials, social media, and other stimulating circumstances or objects, as well as any other environmental temptations, are all part of the sexual surrendering process.

Relational and social surrender- in this situation, addicts realise they have no control over anyone except themselves. Consequently, a person may choose to surrender by avoiding close friendships or relationships who aren't supportive of sobriety. Furthermore, rather than relying on oneself alone, relational surrender emphasised the value of a supporting community and accountability for successful recovery. The best description of this can be found in the Big book of Alcoholics Anonymous (p. 417), which states:

> *"When I am disturbed, it is because I find some person, place, or situation—some fact of my life—unacceptable to me, and I can find no serenity until I accept that person, place, thing, or situation as being exactly the way it is supposed to be at this moment. … Unless I accept life completely on life's terms, I cannot be happy. I need to concentrate not so much on what needs to be changed in the world as on what needs to be changed in me and in my attitudes."*

All relationships are clouded and disturbed by sex addiction. To reconnect and understand relationships with yourself, God or a higher power, you must surrender your relationship with sex addiction first. Relational surrendering also includes having a therapeutic relationship with a trustworthy professional, one-on-one accountability with persons of the same gender, and restored intimate and non-intimate relationships.

Spiritual surrender- is a spiritual act requiring faith and trust. How can someone give up control if they don't trust they'll be safe and cared for? Fear is the polar opposite of faith, and it is the primary barrier that keeps individuals from entering the uncharted territory of surrendering. Because both faith and fear require a person to believe in something they cannot see, the decision of what to believe is left up to the individual. You take a leap of faith and face your fears of the unknown when you declare complete surrender to your God or higher power, which opens the door to endless prospects.

Sex addicts, have a natural lack of trust and faith in others, and instead rely on their own judgement and abilities. This is why some are unable to overcome their addiction. Recovery from sex addiction is the start of a brand new life. A life free of sexual acting out opens up previously unimagined possibilities for personal growth, development, and advancement in all aspects of life. Considering all of the possibilities can help put things into perspective.

Recovering sex addicts need to cultivate a positive mindset and a gratitude attitude in enhancing their trust and faith. For example, rather than simply asking, 'What could possibly go wrong?' They should ask themselves, 'What's the best that could happen?'

Addicts, must refrain from fear and remain faithful, trust the recovery process and continue their spiritual journey into an experience that is vastly different from the devastating, dismal habits they had led when engaging in addictive behaviours.

Fear has no end. When one fear is eliminated, another one replaces it. It is comparable to digging up weeds. Even when all weeds have been eliminated, new ones immediately emerge. It is necessary to uproot the dirt and treat it. To drive out fear, one needs to treat the soul with faith. Consequently, if individuals have a positive attitude and trust that everything will work out, they can enjoy the moment and integrate into their new emerging sober lifestyles.

The goals of spiritual surrender are healing and repair, not absolution of guilt. To break the cycle of sex addiction, spiritual awakening, connection to God or another higher power, and the power of prayer are essential. Some addicts still hope that God or their higher force would strike them in the head via parted clouds, causing a spiritual awakening and subsequent surrender. God or a higher power, has already performed miracles in their life by providing qualified therapists, medical professionals, fellowships, books, and other resources. God or a higher power has already revealed Himself to addicts through all of these support systems on multiple occasions. However, these individuals were not ready to give up lust. They are not ready to:

'simply give up, let go and let God' as it is in the White book' (2016).

Spiritual surrender entails standing aside to allow God or a higher power to perform its magic, but it also entails letting go of attitudes like 'I don't believe in magic and miracles!' that some sex addicts hold. Spiritual surrender, relationship with God or a higher power, and religiousness have been shown to improve health and addiction recovery in numerous scientific studies. It is critical in sex addiction recovery to have a sense of belonging rather than feeling alone.

Spiritual surrender is an important component of recovery, since it allows people to let go of their sense of self, control, ego, self-directive attitude, and rediscover a sense of interconnectedness and belonging. Spiritual surrender also allows us to live in the here and now and become more aware of ourselves as well as our effect on the environment and one another.

Surrender to God's will is another premise important to the Christian concept of surrender. Surrendering to God's will requires both the surrender of our will to His, as well as faith in His sovereignty over all things, in which His ways of functioning and thinking triumph over all (Eph 5:2).

Surrender in Islam, involves relinquishing control and placing total trust in Allah's grand master plan for one's life. Surrender in Buddhism refers to a belief and trust in anything other than one's own ego. Whatever people surrender to – higher power, religion, God, the universe, or simply existence -the key point is that the individuals no longer consider themselves to be in charge and supreme.

'Sometimes surrender means giving up trying to understand and becoming comfortable with not knowing.' Eckhart Tolle

Many people in recovery from sex addiction are unclear of their own spirituality, but they are comfortable identifying a higher power to whom they can surrender.

Surrendering to a higher power also entails being open to new possibilities and realising that one's existing choices aren't getting them anywhere. When a person surrenders to a higher power, it's an indication that they're optimistic about the outcome. Consequently, the prefrontal cortex is forced to participate in a thinking process that was previously dulled by addictive behaviours, which aids in brain regeneration.

It can feel like a loss at first to change and let go of unhelpful coping mechanisms, old patterns of behaviour that don't serve you, and distorted beliefs that fuelled your addiction. Grief is generally associated with loss, and the early stages of surrender might feel like a period of grieving.

Surrender, can lead to joy and liberation when you finally realise and accept what you've known all along but were too afraid to face. When you accept your powerlessness and begin to perceive reality through the perspective of something higher and more powerful than yourself, you may begin to address the problem's true underlying causes instead of denying them.

> *'You learned to run from what you feel….To deny is to invite madness. To accept is to control.'*
>
> *Megan Chance (2008)*

There is no longer a need to control the wants and desires when an addict surrenders and releases their ego to a higher power because they turn their ego and self-will over to a deeper wisdom and knowing inside themselves. They let go of the painful distortions of certainty, contradictions, and separateness as they surrender to a higher self, and embrace the truth of unpredictability, consistency, connection, and wholeness.

PRACTICAL RECOVERY TOOLS

Pause, breathe and surrender the unpleasant thoughts, memories, and emotions. It's crucial to remember that striving to suppress, fight, or flee unpleasant memories or sensations simply reinforces them because they're coming from the unconscious mind. This area of the brain is a part of the brain that is incapable of reasoning.

Surrendering and understanding that triggering thoughts are still just thoughts offers you power. When a trigger arises, all you have to do is become aware of situations, identify your emotions and thoughts, and then let them go. The more you apply this technique, the more likely you are to get relief.

If you gently acknowledge your thoughts and learn to let them go, they will disappear faster. Allowing your thoughts to exist does not imply that you must give them your whole attention or that you must deny them.

Surrender can be unsettling since it might bring up feelings of fear, resentment, righteous anger, and pain. Take it slowly, be gentle with yourself, and be patient as you let go. You must establish a sense of safety, practise self-care, and enlist the support of people you can trust and who support your sobriety.

Examples of how to surrender:

1) Identify your distorted thoughts, feelings and/or triggers. Instead of believing them, challenge them.

   A Sex addicts' ego and self-will confines them, causing them to function at lower levels of consciousness. Surrender, requires a certain level of awareness. A healthy ego is what allows a person to endure in the face of adversity such as loss, disappointment, and other setbacks. Ego distortions like self-will, control, pride, excessive self-image, lack of humility, and grandiosity can make surrender difficult. You can identify what is true and what is distortion by evaluating your beliefs, emotions, and triggers, and thereby enhance your consciousness, which allows you to surrender.

2) Allow some time to rest and pause.

   Recovering addicts are frequently concerned about the outcome of circumstances over which they have little control. It's fine to relax and trust that everything will turn out as it should. Anxiety does nothing but make you miserable because it is a familiar trigger.

3) Consider whether you're motivated by a need for control or by a fear of losing control. Take a deep breath, be present, and consider how and why you're trying to exert control.

4) Take note of where you are.

Ground yourself (use 5 senses grounding technique) by paying attention to your surroundings. Name a few things you can see, smell, touch, or hear. When you're present and aware, you're more likely to experience surrender and gratitude.

5) Cultivate an attitude of unconditional self-compassion and self-love.

Surrendering to a selfless love is extremely powerful, but it is sometimes overlooked. Even if you're experiencing unpleasant emotions, triggers, worry, temptation, resistance, or any other distress, be kind and compassionate to yourself. Always remember that you are deserving of forgiveness and friendship from yourself.

6) Write a loving and forgiving letter to yourself, and read it aloud a few times.

If the concept of doing this makes you uncomfortable or you think it's a silly idea, it's possible that you don't know how to give self-love or self-forgiveness and this is a necessary exercise for you.

7) Surrender prayer can help you reconnect with yourself and a higher power.

This does not have to be a conversation with a specific god if you do not believe, but simply contemplative phrases that you repeat to bring yourself and your thoughts back to the present moment.

Example of surrender prayers:

Father God/ Higher power, I place my addiction challenges in your capable hands. Send spiritual helpers into my life to assist me in discovering my true identity and purpose. Please help me to see myself as a victor rather than a victim. Allow me to begin my recovery journey from a place of triumph and peace, believing that you have already set me free. Amen.

Lord/ higher power, I admit my wrongdoings and am grateful for my growing self-forgiveness. Please help me forgive myself as well as others who have wronged me. Give me a heart that is willing to forgive in order for me to find joy and serenity. Please assist me in regaining my self-love. Allow me to grow in self-love and self-forgiveness to the point where I no longer need to live my life to please others or according to their opinions. Amen.

Creator, please help me to grow in self-love until all of my dreams have been transformed from fear and drama to love and joy. Allow the power of my self-love to shatter all of my unworthiness beliefs and all of the lies I've told myself. Let love be the foundation of all my actions, reactions, thoughts, and emotions from now on. Begin by teaching me to love myself so much that I will never put myself in situations that are harmful to myself or others. Amen.

Lord/higher power, teach me to love myself without passing judgement on myself, for when I do, I pass judgement on others, I carry blame and shame, a desire for vengeance, and I lose sight of your grace. Allow me to cultivate respectful and joyful relationships with others so that I am no longer compelled to control them. Teach me how to welcome the unconditional love that is my inheritance into my heart. Please help me to love myself completely and truly enough to forgive everyone who has ever wronged me as well as myself for my inability to control myself. Assist me in becoming a master of humility and appreciation, compassion, and love, so that I may enjoy all of your gifts in perpetuity. Amen.

Surrender Questions

? What is it that you want? Why do you desire it?

_____

_____

_____

_____

? What are your beliefs regarding what you want or desire?

_____

_____

_____

_____

⑦ I'd like it because

_____

_____

_____

_____

⑦ That's necessary for me to have it because

_____

_____

_____

_____

⑦ If I don't have it, this may happen

_____

_____

_____

_____

Non-negotiable Rules of Recovery

⑦ What would it signify if you weren't able to get what you want?

_____

_____

_____

_____

⑦ What do you think you need to do in order to get what you want?

_____

_____

_____

_____

⑦ Where are you in a fight with life? What are you unwilling to accept and surrender to?

_____

_____

_____

_____

⑦ Do you have the feeling that if you don't have control over others or results, you will never get what you want?

___

⑦ Do you feel supported in your recovery, or do you feel like you are on your own?

___

⑦ Do you know how to relinquish control and surrender? If so, go over each step in detail. If not, what are the problems?

___

Non-negotiable Rules of Recovery

(?) Who or what situations have you tried to exert control over, and how do you plan to give up power?

(?) What frustrates you the most right now in your life? Where are you enforcing your will and way of life? What are your expectations?

⑦ What effect does your forcing or controlling energy have on your body, breath, mood, recovery and relationships?

_____

_____

_____

_____

⑦ When you think about letting go, stepping back, and surrendering, what emotions, thoughts, or images emerge?

_____

_____

_____

_____

⑦ Identify some of your own distorted beliefs or thought patterns about what will happen if you abandon control?

_____

Non-negotiable Rules of Recovery

⑦ Which of these distorted beliefs do you recognise as recurring and familiar themes in your life?

⑦ What benefits do you gain by refusing to surrender? By holding on, what are you avoiding having to do or feel?

(?) In what ways and to what extent have you used control in your life?

_____

_____

_____

_____

(?) You won't let go of control and surrender because you are:

_____

_____

_____

_____

(?) And don't want to feel:

_____

_____

_____

_____

Non-negotiable Rules of Recovery

⁇ What benefits do you gain from surrender?

_____

_____

_____

_____

⁇ Who or where are your safe people or places for experiencing and expressing your feelings regarding what you want, your fears of not getting it, and the potential of surrendering and letting go?

_____

_____

_____

_____

⁇ What are your plans for self-care and consciousness?

_____

_____

_____

_____

⊙ Are your enough, and do you believe that you are enough right now?

_____

_____

_____

_____

⊙ Do you believe that if you use control to get all you desire, you only end up creating big blocks? Explain.

_____

_____

_____

⊙ Would surrendering and letting go feel liberating and empowering? Explain.

_____

_____

_____

_____

Non-negotiable Rules of Recovery

⑦ In your life and recovery, how and through whom and what is your higher power at work?

_____

_____

_____

_____

⑦ Do you have difficulty understanding a higher power? Explain.

_____

_____

_____

_____

⑦ What role does your current understanding of a higher power play in your desire to stay sober?

_____

_____

_____

_____

⑦ What's the difference between your will and the will of a higher power?

_____

_____

_____

_____

⑦ What changes in your life and recovery may you notice if you decide to 'turn it over?'

_____

_____

_____

_____

⑦ What are you in control of?

_____

_____

_____

_____

Non-negotiable Rules of Recovery

⑦ What are you not in control of?

_____

_____

_____

_____

⑦ How do you intend to practice self-love and self-forgiveness?

_____

_____

_____

_____

CHAPTER 12

Things You Can and Cannot Control

The ability to affect or direct people's behaviour or the course of events is characterised as control. Sex addicts engage in a variety of controlling behaviours prior to recovery:

- To compensate for feeling out of control of their sex addiction, an addict may try to exert control over their environment.
- Addicts frequently engage in lying and manipulative behaviours, both of which are methods of controlling others and their reactions. Sex addiction is defined by uncontrollable physical and psychological triggers that

make it difficult for a person to resist urges, regardless of the consequences.
- Sex addiction is an intense preoccupation that consumes a person's thoughts, behaviours, and desires. Nothing else matters in this state, even the well-being and feelings of loved ones. Sexual compulsions and desperation erase all morals, allowing the addict to control others through bizarre sexual demands (i.e., pressuring a partner to join a threesome or have group sex, etc.)
- Individuals may use various strategies to manipulate people in order to achieve their own goals. This may include ensuring that sex addicts are in a position of authority so that they can control and exploit people for their own gain.
- To passively maintain control, sex addicts may avoid others or isolate themselves from friends and loved.
- Anger outbursts, throwing things, slamming doors, and yelling or other intimidating conducts are all examples of controlling behaviours.
- Prior to recovery, sex addicts may seek to exert control over others by threatening to harm or kill themselves in order to elicit a reaction from others.
- They may blame or gaslight loved ones in an attempt to control them and their reality.
- Even during the recovery process, a sex addict may hesitate to offer an honest disclosure in order to control what others think of them.
- Controlling behaviours may occur during therapy and recovery when an individual wants to control the process and resists certain aspects of it because they are out of his control.
- Addicts can use denial in their thinking to keep them in control and prevent them from truly surrendering.

- Individuals' energy might be channelled elsewhere during the recovery process if they realise, they have little control over external events. By relinquishing control over external events, addicts acquire confidence in themselves. Individuals might then focus on the only area of their lives over which they have control: their reactions, thoughts, attitudes, and perspectives. By relinquishing control, individuals will experience increased productivity, joy, confidence at work, and access to unique or exciting choices that they had not before explored. As a result, physical and emotional health increases, as does mental fortitude, mental capacity and self-awareness.

'Incredible change happens in your life when you decide to take control of what you do have power over instead of craving control over what you don't.... The reason many people in our society are miserable, sick, and highly stressed is because of an unhealthy attachment to things they have no control over.'

Steve Maraboli

PRACTICAL RECOVERY TOOLS

STOP and release your control:

Stop what you're doing. Pay attention to yourself and note how much you want to control everything.

Take a breath, pause and focus on your breathing.

Observe your own thoughts, emotions, and physical responses. Allow yourself to practise being observant of what you're attempting to control. Remain aware of your physical sensations, as well as any thoughts or feelings that emerge.

Plan and ponder mindfully about how you'd like to respond. Keep your attention on the present moment, be aware of your surroundings, and treat yourself with love and kindness. When you adopt a grateful, appreciating attitude rather than a worried, anxious, and controlling one, it's easier to accept things as they are and let go of the want to control or be attached to things that aren't beneficial for you.

Stay mindful and develop the practise of accepting that you don't know everything and that you don't have complete

Things You Can and Cannot Control

control. And that's okay. Allow yourself to relax into a state of uncertainty and receptivity to life and just be.

Intentionally, simply observe and see if it's possible to look at something without placing a label on it? Or when you think about it, do you need to categorise it, criticise it, and force a flood of feelings and opinions on it?

Things you can control:	**Things you cannot control:**
Your breathing, mindset, gratitude, behaviours, and belief system.	What others think, say about you or react to you.
Your responses to others.	What other people do or don't do.
Your triggers and emotions.	
Your recovery and sobriety.	What happens unpredictably in life and around the world.
Your values and boundaries.	
Your body language.	What will happen in the future and what has already happened in the past.
Your physical and mental health.	
Your diet, rest and self-care.	Other people's boundaries.
Your relationship with yourself, others, and your body.	The process of ageing and death.

Control Questions:

⑦ What aspects of your life do you have control over?

_____

_____

_____

_____

_____

⑦ What aspects of your life are you unable to control?

_____

_____

_____

_____

_____

Things You Can and Cannot Control

⊙ What aspects of your life have you wrongly sought to control and now need to give up control over?

_____

_____

_____

_____

_____

⊙ How can you create a safe space where you can express your feelings about things you can't control?

_____

_____

_____

_____

_____

_____

⑦ How can you feel in control of your life when you can't walk away from stressful situations without exploding or suppressing?

_____
_____
_____
_____
_____
_____

⑦ How can you take control of your work and finances in a healthy way?

_____
_____
_____
_____
_____
_____

Things You Can and Cannot Control

⑦ Is your schedule the place where you want to feel in control, with the ability to choose your work schedule and travel when and where you want?

_____

_____

_____

_____

_____

⑦ Decide what you need to happen in order to feel in control of what happens in your recovery?

_____

_____

_____

_____

_____

_____

(?) What is the most important thing to you in life? Are you in control of the situation?

_____
_____
_____
_____

(?) What motivates you to keep going in your recovery?

_____
_____
_____
_____

(?) What does it means to you to be 'in control.'

_____
_____
_____
_____

Things You Can and Cannot Control

⑦ Are you ready to let go of the past? Or do you still want to control and modify a few things? Explain.

_____

_____

_____

_____

⑦ Do you frequently consider the future and wish to have some control over certain areas of it? Explain.

_____

_____

_____

_____

⑦ Are you willing to accept your current situation?

_____

_____

_____

_____

⑦ Do you have any controlling attitudes or perspectives that are preventing you from progressing in therapy?

_____

_____

_____

_____

_____

⑦ Do you have any controlling attitudes or viewpoints that are preventing you from making progress in your recovery or sobriety?

_____

_____

_____

_____

_____

_____

Things You Can and Cannot Control

⑦ Identify what attitudes and viewpoints are holding you back in your relationships?

_____

_____

_____

_____

_____

⑦ What parts of your recovery and life do you have control over?

_____

_____

_____

_____

_____

⑦ What parts of your recovery and life do you have NO control over?

_____

_____

? How do you manage your own self-care?

? How would you feel if you were given a mental health evaluation to rule out any other underlying issues that could be driving your sex addiction?

Things You Can and Cannot Control

⑦ Why is it so important to get a full mental health evaluation?

_____

_____

_____

_____

_____

⑦ Do you really believe a higher power loves you and will care for you? Explain.

_____

_____

_____

_____

_____

CHAPTER 13

Spiritual Awakening

If the surrender process is effective, it will eventually result in spiritual awakening which is waking up to self and life. Spiritual awakening is a core element of the soul's development and the breakdown of the fallacy of ego and disconnection. Many people in recovery talk about their spirituality, and many of them attribute their recovery to a spiritual awakening. Let's explore what a spiritual awakening is and how to achieve it while in recovery from sex addiction. It's critical to understand that spirituality is not the same as religiosity, and that spirituality in recovery has a greater purpose.

Being spiritually awakened prevents you from harming, condemning, or categorising others. Instead, you enter a condition of humility where you are conscious of your attachment to God or a higher power and are therefore shielded from outside pressure, judgment or impulses.

Spiritual awakening is a subjective experience in which a person's ego surpasses and transcends their ordinary, limited sense of self to incorporate a broader, unlimited sense of truth or reality. These profoundly embodied, intellectual experiences are sometimes perceived as a direct connection, communion, or consciousness integration with a limitless and global awareness, the divine or 'God,' in experiencing oneness. The experiences that come from the spiritual connection, according to Tanyi (2002), one of the most extensively recognised scholarly publications, include:

> '…. This connection brings faith, hope, peace, and empowerment. The results are joy, forgiveness of oneself and others, awareness and acceptance of hardship and mortality, a heightened sense of physical and emotional well-being, and the ability to transcend beyond the infirmities of existence' (p. 506).

Spiritual awakenings elicit an inexplicable profound experience of inner knowing, acceptance, reminiscing, or discovering one's true character, whether slow or rapid, evoked or unanticipated. Individuals commonly express sentiments such as feelings of peace and serenity, bliss, elation, and vitality, feelings of astonishment, sanctity, appreciation, and faith, and feelings of abundant, and unconditional love. These deep experiences may also result in an increase in physical and emotional reactivity to environmental cues such as colour, light, touch, sound, and scent, as well as a sense of time and space consciousness. These sensitivities can often lead to paranormal-like experiences, with people claiming enhanced spiritual presences, hearing sounds or voices that aren't created externally, and seeing things that aren't physically present.

Spiritual Awakening

Spiritual awakenings can be unnerving at first since they typically leave people questioning what's going on, who they are, and what is their purpose. At the same time, these spiritual experiences can make a person feel incredibly alive, with a sense of wonder and joy.

Spirituality and spiritual awakening, can have a dramatic, positive impact on a person's recovery and is often the cornerstone for effective and permanent sobriety.

Many people have spiritual awakenings and experiences while trying to get sober and working with a therapist and a sponsor. The key to achieving this transformation is to keep an open mind, surrender, be willing to try new things, and be honest with yourself and others. The true nature of the spiritual awakening or experiences vary widely from person to person, and for many spiritual experiences develop over time. Spiritual awakening is a possibility for everyone. It might not always look that way. Some individuals have been so mired in the narrative of their day-to-day existence that they have lost sight of who they truly are. But everyone who strives for consciousness will eventually understand and connect to what their true essence and purpose are.

One type of awakening is slower, like a mild experience that causes you to modify your perspective on life. Small health issues, repeated challenges or failures, recurring cycles of unhealthy behaviours, or any overarching sensation that motivates you to try something new.

The other is a sudden awakening, which is similar to waking up from a dream and realising you aren't in one. You will feel compelled to make drastic and instantaneous changes in your life if you have a sudden awakening, such as when you hit rock bottom during active sex addiction.

Awakening takes time, and the process is constantly evolving to represent the facts of life. This evolutionary process must fundamentally alter ones' consciousness from a false-self to a true-self, from a limited-self to an expanded-self, from a selfish-self to a selfless-self, and from an ignorant-self to a wise-self.

Once the soul awakens and the search begins, there is no going back. You are then overcome with a singular need that keeps you from ever again wandering in a state of helplessness and inadequate wholeness. The spiritual realm will compel you. You will become determined to reach the pinnacle of contentment and will not let fear about getting harmed or being weak stop you.

Despite the fact that this process of consciousness cannot be forced, if you are seeking spiritual awakening, you are already on your way to discovering new dimensions of yourself. True recovery from sex addiction necessitates some spiritual awakening, which allows you to separate from the addiction's thoughts, reconnect with the truth of your soul, and help others.

Spirituality mandates that the purpose of recovery is to look within, examine oneself, determine what is appropriate and necessary, and then take specific and deliberate steps towards it. Prior to recovery, sex addicts believe they can control their compulsive behaviours, and their obliviousness to the truth that they are out of control leads them to greater sexual, physical, psychological, and spiritual dysfunction and distress. Sex addiction erodes the individuals spiritually because compulsive sexual behaviours provide a false sense of purpose, and brain chemicals provide a false sense of value and fulfilment. As a result, when a person stops acting out sexually, they may feel empty and lost.

A person in early recovery can identify with and rely on a power larger than themselves after discovering previously unknown internal assets. Rather than relying on compulsive sexual behaviours to increase dopamine release for validation and a sense of purpose, individuals in recovery are encouraged to connect to a higher power to restore their hope, purpose, and consciousness. This is a process of becoming more cognisant of and conscious of one's inner wisdom voice. The term spiritual awakening is commonly used to describe both the mental and spiritual transformation (consciousness process) and the act of sobriety. This process creates a substantial alteration in one's perspective and experience of life.

Spirituality refers to an inner energy, a power, or a purpose, and is derived from the Latin word 'spiritus,' which means 'breath of life' or 'what gives life, existence.'

Spiritual awakenings can be triggered by a variety of situations, ranging from every day to life-changing. People who open a spiritual door or life-changing circumstances (a sex addict being exposed, losing a job or relationship, a serious accident, near death experience, trauma, depression, etc.) are some examples of the common causes. Relatedly, anything that encourages a person to consider their life from a spiritual perspective may lead to awakening.

PRACTICAL RECOVERY TOOLS

How to facilitate for spiritual awakening?

1) Evaluate your distorted beliefs, broaden your horizons, and clear your physical and emotional clutter to create space for new experiences. An awakening happens when you find something new, and you've essentially aroused your mind and spirit from a state of hibernation to increasing your chances of awakening to a life experience you weren't even aware you were having. You must cultivate an open mind and be receptive to new ideas and perspectives, meditate, read, and talk to others who have had different lives and have remained sober for a long time.

2) Allow yourself to reconnect with nature by spending time in the great outdoors. Take advantage of the serenity, tranquillity, and presence that only being outside can bring. Don't let your phone or the presence of others distract you.

3) Take care of your physical health. Staying connected to yourself and your higher power, whether it's God, the universe, or simply another entity, is as simple as eating healthy and staying active.

4) Practice genuine surrender on a regular basis. Remember that spiritual awakening and surrender are not always one-time events, they are interdependent. The spiritual path is a journey of progress that lasts a lifetime.

5) Learn more about yourself and your thoughts. Expand your tolerance window with effective psychotherapy, reflection, and journaling that forces you to identify and address your own blind spots and distorted belief systems.

6) Engage with people who can inspire you spiritually and develop an attitude of gratitude.

Spiritual awakening is in actuality impossible to classify. It's a non-linear and multi-dimensional process that's unique for everyone. It requires the removal of outward ego, attachments, pain, and other significant variables. Therefore, being inspired by a spiritual person who understands this process is crucial. Find spiritually compatible persons with whom you can connect. A spiritual person's path can inspire, direct, and lead you back to yourself and your recovery.

It's the re-discovery of your true-self that has been buried beneath all of your compulsive sexual behaviours, deceptions, and lies.

Gratitude is a part of a larger perspective on life that includes observing and appreciating the good things in life. It might be attributed to an external source (for example, a pet), a person, or a non-human being (e.g., God). It's also a typical and significant part of spiritual awakening and spirituality. People express gratitude for the positive things in their lives and it allows them to connect to something greater than themselves, whether it's other people, nature, or a higher power.

Recent medical studies have found that those patients who kept gratitude journals for eight weeks seemed to have a more grateful heart that was indeed a more medically healthy heart.

'It is through gratitude for the present moment that the spiritual dimension of life opens up.' – Eckhart Tolle (2004)

Spiritual Awakening

How can you tell whether you're having a spiritual awakening?

Initially, you may feel alone, isolated or detached from people and maybe more connected to nature.

You may initially feel overwhelmed and perplexed, becoming disconnected from things or people you once enjoyed. This is particularly true if the others in your life aren't on the same page as you. Some recovering addicts, discover that they are more connected to nature and less to people.

You've released your attachments, reconsidered your attitudes, and belief system.

Most sex addicts define themselves in terms of their material possessions, such as money, a car, a job, a home, and so on, therefore letting go of attachments is a significant indicator of your awakening. You may develop a strong connection to a new religion or spirituality, or you may even quit your old job to pursue a new interest, but your priorities in life are likely to be different.

Your waking life and dreams have become more vivid.

The significance of your dreams and how they connect to your life will become more evident.

You recognise and respect your own unique path as well as the paths of others.

Persuasion and conflicts are no longer as significant as they once were.

You want to be of service.

As you come to understand that all living things are essentially worthwhile and equal, you will feel compelled to serve others, whether they are humans, animals, or the environment. You may develop an interest in your community or a specific cause. It is vital for you to have a cause you can get behind if you want your life to be meaningful.

Fear of death is eliminated.
When you focus on living in the moment rather than worrying about the unknown future or lamenting the past, death appears to be less terrifying. This could also be related to detachment from attachments. You view death as an inescapable aspect of life, which reduces fear and allows for peace.

Different teachers find you.
Spiritual instructors (strangers or acquaintances, religious or spiritual leaders) may emerge anywhere at any time to teach you, as if you were a student who is ready to receive.

More synchronicity, paranormal occurrences and déjà vu occur to you.
There's a feeling that the cosmos is conspiring to make something happen, similar to premonition. For instance, imagine thinking about someone and then bumping into them the next day. Some individuals view these signs as coincidences, while others believe they are directing the individuals in the right direction.

The dynamics of your relationships begin to change.
Spiritual awakenings are life-changing, and the people in your life may not always understand this.

Spirituality is becoming increasingly essential in your life, and it leads to inner peace.
As you go through this process, it will be difficult to avoid the appeal from your spiritual self. One of your top concerns will almost certainly be to find purpose, fulfilment, and inner peace in your spirituality. When you have inner peace, it's like being resilient. However, inner peace does not ensure that life will be stress-free; it only implies that you will not experience extreme emotional dysregulation and reactivity when life gets difficult.

You have a stronger intuition, authenticity and can immediately identify deception and dishonesty.

You're discovering new inner resources or enhanced intuition that makes it easier to spot untrustworthy people. A strong sense of self-worth, conviction, and a diminished desire to please people accompany a spiritual awakening. Instead, a genuine attitude of eternal gratitude with who you are and the choices you make emerge.

You become more mindful, present, observe your old patterns, and have a new perspective on the world.

Observation is one of the first indicators of awakening. Because as an addict, you've spent your life oblivious to who you are, what you want, or why you're here. As you become more attuned in the here and now, your habits and routine will abruptly change. You may place a high value on spending time in nature or meditating, or you may be intentionally replacing old habits that weren't serving you well.

You gain more empathy, and compassion for others.

As you become more attuned to the world around you, you will develop a greater empathy for others' pain. In turn, empathy induces an action-oriented compassion. Therefore, you'll be more compassionate and attentive to others while maintaining healthy values and boundaries.

You are surrendering more.

Even if you've recovered and found a way of life that works for you, there may still be individuals or behaviours that are preventing you from moving forwards. You'll realise you need to let go of them in order to truly accept your destiny. Surrendering entails letting go of any lingering ego structures, beliefs, or traits that are preventing you from experiencing your reality and recovering effectively.

Spiritual Awakening Questions:

⑦ When you become aware of your unhealthy habits. Do you find yourself repeating the same patterns again and again?

_____

_____

_____

_____

⑦ What differences have you seen between now and previously in your empathy and compassion for others?

_____

_____

_____

_____

⑦ Is your spiritual progress being aided by your new beliefs and self-awareness? Explain.

_____

_____

Spiritual Awakening

_____

_____

⑦ How long have you been on your spiritual journey? What have been the most difficult challenges you've had to overcome in your journey?

_____

_____

_____

_____

_____

⑦ When someone asks how you're feeling, you usually say…

_____

_____

_____

_____

⁇ Are you fascinated by the things in life that have no easy scientific explanation? Explain.

_____

_____

_____

_____

⁇ Have you had any spiritual experiences that may be difficult for others to understand? Give examples.

_____

_____

_____

_____

⁇ Do you feel connected to nature, as if you're a part of a single living entity, or do you feel detached?

_____

Spiritual Awakening

_____

_____

_____

_____

⓪ Have you ever heard your phone ring and you knew who it was before looking?

_____

_____

_____

_____

⓪ Do you find yourself content with things that would normally bother you? Give examples.

_____

_____

_____

_____

⑦ Have you stopped gossiping? Explain.

_____

_____

_____

_____

⑦ Identify some of your expectations that may be blocking your awakening?

_____

_____

_____

_____

⑦ Identify some of your past wounds, shortcomings, or reluctance to forgive that may be preventing you from spiritual awakening?

_____

_____

_____

_____

Spiritual Awakening

⁇ How are you consistent and resilient in your spiritual practices?

_____

_____

_____

_____

⁇ Are you responding or reacting to situations and people you don't like?

_____

_____

_____

_____

⁇ Define what inner peace means to you?

_____

_____

_____

_____

⑦ Do you have a fear of dying? Explain.

_____
_____
_____
_____

⑦ What areas of your life do you still compare yourself to others in? How do you feel about that?

_____
_____
_____
_____

⑦ Have you let go of your attachments, such as material possessions, ego, and so on? Explain.

_____
_____
_____
_____

CHAPTER 14

Love and Lust

Before and throughout recovery, sex addicts appear to be perplexed by the concepts of love and lust. This chapter will explain them in terms of sex addiction.

What is love?

Experiencing love is one of the most joyous aspects of being human. Although there isn't a single definition for love, it is generally understood to be a strong sense of affinity, ardour, and warmth towards another person. Love, according to Dr. Robert Sternberg's research, is a set of emotions and behaviours marked by intimacy, passion, and commitment. Compassion, intimacy, nurturance, desire, respect, and trust are all involved. Both biological and cultural variables, as well as our own choices, are likely to influence our love for one another. While hormones and genetics have a role, our personal beliefs of love have an impact on how we decide to express and experience love.

Seeking and finding love is a natural element of human nature. Romantic love has been discovered in all civilizations, implying that love has a fundamental biological component. Culture can have a tremendous impact on how people perceive, encounter, and display love. Romantic love, sometimes known as love, is a physiological force that has come to be understood as an emotion, motivation, decision, and an action by society.

Emotional responses include euphoria, intense focus on a chosen individual, obsessively thinking about them, emotional reliance on and yearning for emotional connection with this desired, and increased energy.

Romantic love activates a motivation system involving brain areas associated with incentive to acquire a reward, rather than being a distinct emotion in and of itself. As a result, love is required for brain homoeostasis, which has ramifications for long-term survival.

Love can provide many benefits, but it usually does so only after a significant amount of effort and perseverance. Love necessitates a decision to cultivate the initial sentiments of attraction, feeding and strengthening them in order to withstand future trials and tribulations. Over time, love can deepen and evolve. It can elicit positive emotions such as joy, enthusiasm, overall happiness, and pleasure, as well as negative emotions like resentment and tension. Love, after all, incorporates wellness, feelings of joy and is a pleasurable and beneficial activity.

Love and Lust

Love is characterised by a deep emotional connection that deepens over time as a result of multiple openly vulnerable and supporting behaviours, and also by a number of deliberate actions that strengthen the intimacy and foster love. In fact, the lack of love may be the root cause of psychopathology and its more severe side effects, such as suicide and femicide*.

Love has a variety of positive effects:

- Diminished heart disease.
- Improved relationship quality and satisfaction.
- Decreased risk of dying from a heart attack.
- Healthier pattern of behaviours.
- Strengthens one's capacity for memory and attention.
- A longer lifespan and less stress.
- Reduction in depression.
- Reduced risk of diabetes.
- Enhanced emotional health.

Love requires respect and trust

Respect is universal and cross-cultural, and it has been defined as the foundation of love. It is crucial in all aspects of interpersonal relationships. It is, necessary for relationship quality and fulfilment, as well as intimacy and connection.

Respect, is a complex neurobiological phenomenon and fosters trust. Love activates certain reward system regions in the brain, resulting in lower emotional judgement and fear and increases trust. In fact, trust can foster greater intimacy, boost attachment and

---

* Femicide refers to the intentional death of women or girls because they are female, as well as the murder of women by close friends or family members.

bilateral exclusivity, and encourage people to lower their defences because they feel safe. Love is impossible to achieve without trust, which is essential for relational intimacy and nurturing. When trust and respect are combined, they can help to facilitate attitude compatibility, mutual self-disclosure and increase attachment.

The sex addict is willing to be sexually fulfilled by any person or by oneself, which renders compulsive sexual behaviour maladaptive and incompatible with love since they lack genuine attachment or closeness. A sex addict might experience feelings of love and even fall in love, but they cannot truly love until they have overcome their addiction and healed themselves. Sex addiction rarely occurs in isolation and commonly co-occurs with other mental health conditions. For instance, the idea of love can be particularly difficult for sex addicts who have autism, whether they have been diagnosed with it or not or are otherwise on the autistic spectrum.

These individuals find it difficult to be intimate, read the cues of love from other people or express love.

What is lust?

Physical excitation is commonly linked to lust, or intense sexual attraction. Wikipedia's definition for lust is more accurate and superior:

Lust can emerge as a comparison and a feeling of resentment. A strong yearning that permeates the entire body is called lust.

Any number of ways, such as the desire for sex, a lavish lifestyle, or power, can be used to express the lust. It can appear in less dramatic ways, such the desire for food rather than a need for it.

Lust is sometimes referred to as coveting. Money, power, celebrity, control, food, or, in the majority of our situations, sex in its various forms, may all make you feel as though you can never have enough of anything. A common human emotion, lust also occurs outside of romantic relationships. Lust is a sensation of urges or ideas that are sexual in nature; healthy people do not always act on these urges or thoughts.

Uncontrolled lust is an intense desire that can drive people to act against their better judgement in an effort to appease their cravings. Moreover, lust is the part of a person who is just interested in pleasure, in temporarily satiating their physical, emotional, and sexual needs, and not interested in a love connection.

Then, lust becomes incredibly individualised, self-centred, and focused on how it makes the person feel physically, even though it is fleeting. Even after fulfilling their sexual objectives, these individuals are still drawn to other people through lust.

The parts of the brain that control pleasure emotions, such as sex-related emotions and the desire to experience sexual fulfilment from another person, are activated by lust.

Lust is the driving force behind a sex addict's behaviour and characterised by an unquenchable desire for sex rather than an excessive liking of sex.

> 'Lust is the killer for a sex addict. 'Lust kills the spirit . . . Lust kills me' (White Book, 2016,).

Sex addicts often struggle in their attempts to stop lusting while in recovery and wonder if it is even possible to look at other attractive people without doing so. The answer is that if you fall into this category, you have no alternative but to completely eliminate lust from your life due to a severe allergy. Your sex addiction is fed by this allergy, which ultimately kills you. Lust-fuelled living is meaningless and leaves you feeling unfulfilled all the time. It disconnects you from reality by keeping your focus on your ego and what you lack.

While character flaws are natural components of being human, lust is a conscious act. People frequently rationalise away their defects and attribute their actions to human weakness or other external causes in order to keep up their destructive behaviour. But being weak and human doesn't mean you should give up trying to rise above your primal desires. You shouldn't act on impulses and feed the ego just because you feel like it, especially if doing so may jeopardise your health or the wellbeing of others.

What is progressive victory over lust?

Lust is the driving force behind our sexual acting out, and true sobriety includes *'progressive victory over lust'*, according to Sexaholics Anonymous, a 12-step recovery fellowship. Progressive victory over lust is ambiguous and sometimes harder to describe than not having sex with self or others, although addicts are aware and cunning of how to challenge even that. The sentence is ultimately interpreted differently by many people.

Addiction develops and escalates over time. The White Book (2016) says:

> '…. sexaholism doesn't stand still; it *progressively* worsens.' (p. 32).

Love and Lust

In order to realise the promise of progressive recovery, you must continue making progress. The expression 'progressive victory over lust' is abused when you give into a brief period of deliberate temptation, such as catching a glance of the person or object out of the corner of your eye. Consequently, there is no such thing as a progressive victory at that point because either you take heroin, or you don't.

Progressive victory over lust does not imply that you lust less and less over time; and hopefully one day you stop lusting; rather, it implies that you quit lusting completely and promptly, which will gradually and progressively become easier.

A heroin addict cannot gradually beat heroin addiction by doing less and less each day until he is miraculously cured one day. Stopping lust is as intentional as starting it. Loren (2017) says that 'Lusting…. is like riding a roller coaster. Once started, it is nearly impossible to stop. Therefore, lust must be stopped where it begins…

> 'Getting out from under the influence of lust, therefore, would require us to avoid getting on board in the first place.' (p. 20).

You've got to become aware of your propensity to let your eyes wander or how easily a fantasy might take root in your head. Each time you have a lustful thought, you must choose to entertain it by making a deliberate choice to do so. This time, it can't be a case of doing just a little bit since every time you do, you expose yourself to a fatal allergy. Additionally, each time you choose to take a little bit of lust, you reinforce the previous neuropathway pattern in the brain, making it harder to break such habits and delaying effective recovery. You are hindering your tranquillity by giving up the dream of a peaceful existence in favour of a fleeting, harmful illusion of pleasure.

As the victory over lust develops, devious lust which is crafty, and perplexing delivers a wider variety of tricks. Surrendering lust means deciding to never engage in a particular act or thought again. Otherwise, the process stops being progressive and becomes unproductive. When a partner isn't around, lust may appear as a voice that says, 'This time, you know how to manage it, so a little online browsing or porn won't hurt.' Or 'checking your news feed, reading celebrity gossip, or browsing Instagram aren't really harmful to your recovery. Or your discussion with someone at the grocery store grows into a flirtatious, funny exchange, to which lust responds, 'You're just being polite and a nice person, surely this is okay'. Lust could entice you to peek in case you know the individual who passes by or says, 'You're not even interested because she or he is not even your type.' In either case, lust drives you to indulge, pass judgement, and objectify. Most sex addicts require a straightforward, binary path to follow. They are adept at pushing and crossing lines. Whatever they do, they can always find a way to justify it by claiming that they are still sober and that their behaviours are sobriety friendly. Regardless of your justifications, you either lust or you don't whenever that image, fantasy, or memory strikes. It is totally impossible to try to stop lusting one little bit at a time (or so called progressive victory over lust). There is no middle ground or compromise.

In *'Keys to recovery,'* author Roy K highlights his own ongoing victory over lust. He does not outline a sometimes-does, sometimes-doesn't progression in it. Instead, he describes how he over time found new examples of lust in his life. These weren't brand-new in the sense that they had never been a part of his life or way of thinking, but they were new to him. And a smouldering attitude was applied to every discovery. For instance, he talks about how he discovered lust in his marriage bed and how he realised he required lust in the form of imagination to keep his arousal with his wife. Lust! He goes on to say that overcoming this recently discovered lust was a lengthy, sluggish procedure. Also known as a year of abstinence. This lust-related manifestation was found, identified, and removed.

The White Book of Sex Addiction (2016) explicitly states that *'Progressive victory'* over character defects is the power of God or a higher power at work in everyone. In reality, sex addicts fight their old selves, the evil power to which they are inevitably vulnerable, and the force that is always capable of causing harm to others.

A mind of a sex addict always starts with a little bit and progresses to a lot more. Additionally, you 'lack a functioning moderation switch' if you are a sex addict; this is the nature of sex addiction. Since your type of allergy is not treatable by the EpiPen, which healthy individuals use in case of an allergic shock, the only option to protect yourself is to simply decide not to start lusting, even a little bit.

Denial, suppression, or will powering it is just another avoidance strategy used by some well-meaning sex addicts and may even be worse than deliberately indulging in lust. Instead of promoting freedom, suppression increases fear. And it's all stored up in the subconscious, where it gathers steam and eventually explodes in dreams, or shows up in other forms, like resentment, self-hatred or evolves into a different addiction.

Sometimes, you might think that your efforts to induce denial have been successful. However, the lust is still present and intensifying internally as it waits for the ideal opportunity to erupt. That hardly qualifies as a surrender. In reality, suppressing lust just puts it on hold; it cannot be completely defeated.

Many sex addicts think it is wrong to even be tempted and that they shouldn't be tempted in the first place. There is nothing to be afraid of in lust and being tempted does not need to be a frightening or unpleasant experience. Being tempted is not wrong, entertaining and giving into lust and temptation is.

Human sexuality is an important aspect of a sophisticated design that was bestowed upon us, not a dreadful perversion of sex that lust and sex addiction have long made it out to be. Because of this, conquering lust requires conquering distorted sexuality and winning the victory of a real, developed, and wholesome sexuality that doesn't hurt oneself and others. You must simultaneously surrender any lustful thoughts or cravings while not condemning yourself for any triggers or personal flaws. Otherwise, this actually increases your propensity to gravitate towards the thing you're hoping to prevent.

When you come to the realisation that your actual day-to-day activities matter more than your calendar sobriety, you are truly on the road to recovery. The ability to reflect on past behaviour and acknowledge that each time you were tempted, you took concrete action to address it rather than repressing or dreading it, is necessary for progressive recovery from lust. Planning ahead, rehearsing in your head, and becoming as ready as you can for tempting situations in advance are necessary for this. The drive to carry out the next right course of action increases with each win over lust. The next time you experience a lustful thought or image pause a second and calmly acknowledge your allergy before gently turning away.

Stop resisting lust out of fear, shame or condemnation since doing so will just give it more control over you. Your ambition to conquer lust demonstrates your tenacity to defy giving in to weakness and work towards a more positive way of life. This requires all forms of lust, especially lusting after others, to be abandoned by anyone who wants to live a life of truth. A better way of life is being advanced through this deliberate effort.

When lust knocks on your door

- Unless you can once more feel the sensation of ease and comfort that comes with taking a few lust shots, you feel anxious, agitated, and uncomfortable.

- Because lust is a ravenous consumer, you feel like you lose any sense of independence and the capacity to say 'no' to its requests.

- Because of your lust allergy, your body reacts to lust in a way similar to an allergic reaction. You must first experience the urges and give in to them, though, before you can begin to lust.

- Once you've indulged and fed any lust that is devious, perplexing, and strong in nature, quitting becomes nearly impossible. So, it would be wiser not to start.

- Your 'progressive victory over lust' is therefore false and distorted if you are fooled into thinking that you may have the joyful, happy life of recovery if you will simply lust less and less over time and can have occasional small amounts of calculated and well controlled lust (another fallacy of sex addiction). This is similar to a sex addict who believes that he can resume masturbating or viewing some images after a period of calendar sobriety as long as he controls and moderates them. You wouldn't be a sex addict if you were able to manage any of these behaviours, right?

- A change in attitude in your heart and thoughts must therefore be the first and only line of defence against a lust seduction. If your pre-temptation attitude is one of surrender and a commitment to stop lusting, it will be there before you are even tempted.

Love vs Lust

Love	Lust
It is about passion intimacy and commitment, and sometimes sexual.	It is always sexual and about sexual attraction.
Sex is a component of a loving relationship, not its main objective.	Being preoccupied with a person's physical appearance and body.
Desire to spend hours conversing with the partner.	Being more eager to engage in sexual activity than conversation.
Genuinely displaying vulnerability to the other person and investing in their feelings and well-being.	Lust is physically motivated.
	Unwilling to talk about their deeper emotions or future.
Love is emotionally motivated.	There is no genuine desire to spend time together outside of the bedroom.
Gradual interest and integration into each other's lives.	Lust says 'it's about me' or 'I want you'.
Love says 'it's about us' or 'I want us'.	Involves sexual fantasies and desires.
Evolves over time through self-disclosure and the sharing of experiences.	Lust is about taking and is self-centred.
	Lust is rather easy to direct onto another person.

Love and Lust

Love is about giving and is selfless. Love is difficult to immediately direct towards another person.	Although it can seem overwhelming, lust nearly always fades away with time.
Love is long term. Love feels like security and respect because of brain chemicals.	Long-term sustainability is impossible with the tremendous passion of the honeymoon stage.
Love has the capacity to endure.	Relationship issues are difficult for lust to overcome.
Love is about emotional, sexual, spiritual intimacy.	Lust is about physical and sexual intimacy.

PRACTICAL RECOVERY TOOLS

How to win over lust?

To prevent inducing your fight, flight, or freeze response and impairing your ability to make informed decisions, take a few deep breaths and relax. After calming down your nervous system, decide what steps will help you shift your attention and focus. When lust strikes, you might need to use more than one resource to overcome it.

- Using rubber band technique.
- Stop compulsions repetition.
- Avoid entertaining lusty ideas or other triggers.
- Protect your eyes.
- Practise trigger management.
- Ongoing therapy.
- Journaling and reflecting.
- Discuss it with your support network.
- Practice honesty and bring your crafty, secretive inner sex addict to light.
- Prayers.
- Counting backwards from 100 to 0.
- Surrender.
- Step work.

Love and Lust Questions:

⑦ What differentiates lust from love as a relationship starts to take shape?

_____

_____

_____

_____

⑦ When you were dating someone in the past, did you care about them or was it just lust? Explain.

_____

_____

_____

_____

⑦ How might the nature of a relationship affect its outcome—lust or love?

_____

_____

? Do you picture yourself with your current partner in the future Or are you more interested in this individual sexually?

? How did you justify your lusting in the past?

Love and Lust

⑦ Will you ever be able to control how others dress, or what is shown on TV which can make you lustful? Explain.

_____

_____

_____

_____

⑦ How can you tell if someone has your attention because of love or lust?

_____

_____

_____

_____

⑦ What is your definition of progressive victory over lust?

_____

_____

_____

_____

⊙ Is progressive victory over lust necessary?

_____

_____

_____

_____

⊙ Do you believe that, in the future, you will be able to look at people—women or men—without fear, lust, or temptation?

_____

_____

_____

_____

⊙ Do you think that long periods of calendar sobriety can allow you to have wandering eyes?

_____

_____

_____

_____

Love and Lust

⑦ Can you lust a little bit at the time until you fully stop? Explain.

_____

_____

_____

_____

⑦ Where or how in your life right now does lust manifest itself?

_____

_____

_____

⑦ Do you keep entertaining lust and trigger material when it shows up in the real world or in the media?

_____

_____

_____

_____

(?) When fantasies or lustful memories surface, do you indulge in them? Do you intentionally think about them, get high off of them, feed them, or allow them to play?

_____

_____

_____

_____

(?) Identify when and how you actively seeked out objects or people to lust after?

_____

_____

_____

_____

(?) In your opinion why do recovering sex addicts have erotic dreams?

_____

_____

Love and Lust

⑦ Do you have erotic dreams? How often?

⑦ Are you comfortable to protect your eyes when you come across a trigger while with your spouse, partner, or friend? Explain.

? Do you believe you can still entertain some lust? If that's the case, what types of lust do you still allow, and why?

___

? Do you ever have fantasies about leaving your spouse and finding someone else? Explain.

___

? Do you often have the same or similar dreams or memories? Describe them.

___

Love and Lust

_____

_____

_____

_____

⁇ Do you desire the attention of others or to be lusted after?

_____

_____

_____

_____

⁇ Do you now hold any subtle lust items or media?

_____

_____

_____

_____

⁇ Do you avoid having a meaningful physical relationship with your spouse or dating others because you're confused about lust vs love?

_____

_____

_____

_____

_____

⁇ Describe the relationship between your lust and possible emotions like hatred, fear, resentment, and unforgiveness. Or any other distressing emotions.

_____

_____

_____

_____

_____

Love and Lust

(?) When or how did you give in to lust? How much control does it have over you? What control do you possess over it?

(?) Are you attempting to engage in spiritual fellowship with unsurrendered people?

CHAPTER 15

Why Boundaries?

Setting boundaries will be a crucial part in the sex addiction recovery process and an important life skill, regardless of how you choose to continue. A boundary is something that restricts and limits. Boundaries are similar to fences around neighbours which offer the connection's parameters. Contrary to popular belief, barriers do not prevent people from interacting. Instead, they provide safety and order, describe appropriate and inappropriate behaviour in the relationships, and facilitate guidance on how to respond when inappropriate or destructive behaviour occurs. Having clear boundaries demonstrates your self-worth and commitment to recovery.

Our boundaries are established based on our unique needs and values, providing us the freedom to express who we are as people and what matters most to us. They also offer individualised rules for explaining our behaviour to others. Your perception of boundaries is influenced by your upbringing. People rely on the moral standards that are imposed on them by their societal, cultural, and occasionally unwritten rules of behaviour within their family system.

Boundaries begin in childhood, and they frequently last a lifetime. An addict's early life experiences are frequently the source of their boundary problems. Perhaps you were raised with strict rules that caused you to repress your emotions and desire distant relationships. Parents that are too strict and rigid with their children prevent them from growing up and being independent. These kids could become overly dependent on others. An inability to understand and respect healthy boundaries, commonly leads to co-dependent** relationships, sex addicts are frequently the targets of manipulation by others or the manipulators of others.

It is possible that you grew up without any boundaries in your home and lacked the skills and knowledge necessary to forge a sense of identity or self-worth in that environment. The ability to express emotions, ask for assistance, or relate to others in a positive and productive way is lacking in children who have grown up with parents or other caregivers who were inattentive, failed to establish clear boundaries, or did not exhibit how to have a healthy emotional attachment.

Healthy boundaries require maturity, which is the ability to think, articulate, and act in a way that preserves your sense of dignity. When you're stressed or angry, how you set and maintain boundaries shows how mature you are. Clear and healthy boundaries are formed that permit people to express who they are while also allowing

---

** Co-dependency is the term used to describe a person's mental, emotional, physical, and/or spiritual dependence on a spouse, friend, or relative.

others to be themselves in order to ensure emotional, mental, and physical stability.

Why is it important to have boundaries?

It is difficult for sex addicts to understand boundaries, and implementing them into practise is even more challenging. These could be at least in part a result of the fact that most sex addicts are people-pleasers and want external validation in order to prevent social rejection. They may have grown up in dysfunctional family systems without healthy boundaries, thus lacking proper blueprints.

Self-respect matters while expressing and enforcing your boundaries with other people. You'll feel better about yourself if you're direct, honest, and respectful. Additionally, when you avoid conflict while speaking your truths, people are more likely to pay attention to you and not take offence. To let others know which behaviours are acceptable and which are not, one must establish, communicate and implement boundaries. Even though the affected person may still react to your boundary, if you are setting a healthy boundary out of self-care or concern for your sobriety, it is easier to accept the response without seeking to change or correct it.

A boundary that is not upheld out of concern for other people's reactions is not a boundary at all. The person needs to be able to express to their former friends their sobriety boundaries as soon as they commence recovery. These might be in relation with the words used, with sexist or sexual language, or with the display of triggering imagery that these people would try to expose the recovering addict to. Most importantly, it is not the duty of the recovering addict how the boundaries are received and addressed. However, it is one hundred percent and entirely up to the recovering addict to decide whether or not to maintain their relationship with these people.

Addiction is characterized by the absence of awareness and application of healthy boundaries. Recovery calls for a commitment to the basics with boundaries. Therefore, sex addicts in recovery must establish boundaries about their environment, the people they interact with, their use of technology, their language choices, how they spend their time, how they handle challenging emotions, and many other factors. Setting personal boundaries involves responding to oneself. Without defined boundaries, you can occasionally resort to old unhealthy coping mechanisms as a result of your own triggers and emotional reactions.

When boundaries are established and upheld to protect others while avoiding manipulation or exploitation of you, true recovery can begin and advance.

Healthy boundaries

Recovering addicts have a greater risk of acting out or relapsing if they experience too much discomfort. An addict's identity is negatively influenced, leading to discomfort and low self-esteem, when they say yes but their body and soul are really telling no. Healthy boundaries must be established and maintained in order to display that you are protecting your values and respecting those of others. This will help you feel good about yourself and your recovery process.

Healthy boundaries are all about respecting and honouring the needs, wants, and responsibilities of both parties in the relationship. Additionally, relationship abuse can be avoided by maintaining healthy boundaries. It's important to remember that creating and sustaining healthy boundaries requires discipline and intention.

Healthy boundaries consist of:

- Respect for oneself and others. With respect, a recovering addict can have the courage to take responsibility for their thoughts, feelings and behaviours.
- Standing your ground despite disagreement from others and to feel confident expressing emotions in a calm, strong manner without feeling compelled to please. Maintaining personal values, integrity and refusing to conform to social expectations are all examples of healthy boundaries.
- Expressing one's needs in a respectful, clear, and assertive manner.
- Carefully weighing the advantages and disadvantages of being in a relationship.
- Being confident of preserving one's values, morals and convictions despite the opinions of others. In other words, you stop acting like a chameleon and start discovering your true self.
- Pre-plan to maintain boundaries and avoid triggers. In the early stages of recovery, triggers can be people, places, or events. It's imperative to be honest with yourself regarding the places and people who are sobriety friendly or not. It will be simpler to resist temptation if boundaries are established early on and respected.
- Avoiding people pleasing behaviours. Create clear boundaries for your communication abilities. You may struggle to communicate openly and meaningfully in the early stages of your recovery due to intense emotional instability. Setting boundaries will help you better understand your wants and needs and how to interact with others in a healthy way that is based on respect rather than pleasing.

- Creating a sense of worth through establishing mindful trust with people. Poor self-worth and self-esteem are common among recovering addicts, which make them untrusting of other people and prone to making poor choices. Setting boundaries will enable you to create a feeling of identity and value and can improve your self-trust, which will raise your level of mindful trust in others.
- The capacity to refuse requests for favours and activities that would interfere with sobriety and to say 'no' to them. Saying no can be extremely difficult, especially in the beginning stages of recovery. Although you secretly know you need to say no occasionally, you want to feel accepted by others. You are valuing your needs and wants as well as your own self-worth by practising saying no.
- Providing healthy control over one's life. Addicts frequently lack the communication abilities needed to convey desired boundaries or have previously struggled to voice when such boundaries have been breached. Addicts in recovery have a sense of control over their lives because of boundaries, which helps them maintain their independence and build healthy relationships. Without healthy boundaries, it will be difficult to cultivate positive connections with oneself and others.

Sex addiction is fundamentally about the absence of healthy boundaries and the presence of unhealthy ones.

Unhealthy boundaries:

Unhealthy boundaries stem from early life experiences. Children learn that love depends on and is always subject to irrational or changeable rules when they are made to put up with their parents' bad behaviour.

Why Boundaries?

Consequently, they behave like they have no desires or needs, and supress their true-selves. Because they are unable to express their true feelings or say no, these children frequently fear rejection. As a result, they never understand what a healthy boundary is or feels like. Instead, any boundaries they might try to establish end up being destroyed.

As adults, these individuals typically find themselves in intimate relationships, business alliances, and friendships where they are taken advantage of and mistreated on many multiple levels, including physically, emotionally, psychologically, and even sexually. Additionally, these people also are violating others' boundaries and taking advantage of them.

Individuals who regularly maintain unhealthy boundaries experience pain and suffering as opposed to happiness or joy with others and with themselves, even though it seems natural to them. Since things have always been this way for them, people are just unaware of what they are unaware of.

The main cause of unhealthy boundaries or a lack of them is fear. Saying no is difficult for you, and when you do, you generally feel bad. You typically expect to lose something when you have problems saying 'no,' such as acceptability, position, a relationship, future opportunities, or anything comparable.

Prior to entering recovery, sex addicts lack many meaningful relationships due to unhealthy boundaries. They've probably also heard that they tend to be either loud, unpleasant, demanding, or disrespectful, or on the other hand, silent, distant, or quietly resentful and hostile. People in their lives find it difficult to trust them since they prefer to manipulate and deceive others rather than love and respect them.

Lack of clarity on your boundaries makes it difficult for others to respect them, which leads them to intentionally or unintentionally taking advantage of you. This is another reason why unhealthy boundaries are a major cause of relationship dysfunctions.

When your boundaries are violated, you feel a variety of negative emotions, such as anxiety, frustration, shame, and hostility. You may begin to believe that you are less valued than other people and feel mistreated or exploited. Unhealthy boundaries can have negative long-term implications. You may start to feel overwhelmed because you keep putting other people before yourself. You may feel guilty for not appreciating yourself and for allowing others to dictate to you. Consequently, you can feel demotivated to engage in life and perhaps start to experience severe despair as you grow more and more irate, resentful, and unhappy. One could become so exhausted and consumed with the lives and acts of others that they lose focus on their own. Sex addicts with unhealthy boundaries often become resentful when someone crosses their boundaries, especially if they reject or suppress their own emotions, which is a normal response for them. Their relationships will consequently deteriorate and become increasingly strained.

Recognizing and accepting your unhealthy boundaries may be difficult. You are conscious of the fact that you have not always treated people with the courtesy, honour, and compassion that you would hope to be shown in return. Shame and remorse can frequently surface when recovering addicts realise that they are violating boundaries. It is possible that you can unlearn the unhealthy personal boundaries and disrespect for others' boundaries that you have grown accustomed to.

Identifying that you have unhealthy boundaries and that you need to create healthy ones is the first and frequently most difficult step in

Why Boundaries?

building healthy boundaries. Acknowledging the problem gives you the opportunity to find better ways to manage your shortcomings.

Unhealthy boundaries consist of:
- Establishing relationships without considering how recovery may be affected.
- Impulsive behaviours, particularly in intimate relationships.
- Joining dating websites in an effort to start a new relationship while trying to maintain sobriety.
- Disregarding your own beliefs in order to win the approval and satisfaction of others.
- Ignoring one's own triggers and interacting with those who aren't sobriety friendly.
- Either trust everyone, or don't trust anyone.
- Wanting others to understand your needs and wants without communicating them.
- Detrimental self-talk, including belittling yourself, negative language, actions, and thoughts about oneself.
- Disrespecting others' boundaries and acting in a controlling or manipulative manner.
- Allowing others to manipulate you, undermining your sobriety.
- Belittling or shaming others for their beliefs, emotions or pace of their recovery.
- Disrespecting another person's ideals, beliefs, or opinions when you don't agree with them.
- Having trouble saying 'no' or not accepting it when others do.
- Having a sense of responsibility for other people's emotions, happiness or even relapse.
- Needing to 'cure' or 'save' other people.
- Hugging or touching others without their consent.
- Placing yourself in an environment where temptation is likely to occur.

Dr. Fai Seyed Aghamiri

Why is scheduled masturbation detrimental to a recovering sex addict's sobriety?

Any addiction must be conquered with established boundaries and a clear understanding of the concept of sobriety. But for a recovering sex addict, it can perhaps be more challenging to define sobriety. Sexual sobriety is rarely viewed as being the total cessation of sex, even recovering persons who are in committed relationships may practise complete sexual abstinence for small periods of time while gaining perspective or addressing their particular issues.

Sexual sobriety is often defined by the contract a sex addict makes with themselves, their therapist, pastor, and the recovery support system. These agreements often referred to as sex plans or sobriety plans include specific, illustrative behaviours that the sex addict has decided to forego in order to define real sobriety. They are typically in writing. However, sex addicts who haven't fully surrendered their powerlessness continue to utilise the old, flawed belief system (**Addiction Thinking = Stinking Thinking**) where they leave room for themselves to still have their cake and eat it too.

Unfortunately, some well-intentioned therapists or sponsors continue to let the addict choose how much of their fix (which is comparable to alcohol or heroin) they want to take, as long as it is less than what it was before and is planned. Their erroneous mentality enables them to manipulate recovery and introduce things that are self-serving and ensure the addiction continues to thrive. This means that occasionally they define some sexual behaviours (such as regulated and well-controlled masturbation) while actually bringing their own ego-serving, man-made definition. Comparable to convincing yourself that you could be a bit pregnant but in reality, you are either pregnant or you are not. In a same sense, you cannot be a little alcoholic. As such, these individuals have twisted the term surrender and have introduced their own distorted definition of sobriety. Consequently, there is a constant struggle to remain lust-free and truly sober, which consistently results in a flat tyre type of recovery.

Non-compulsive masturbation can occasionally help the biological desire for sexual gratification, provide a short-term outlet for self-nurturance, and offer an objective sense of sexual health in a healthy person. However, the same story is not true for a sex addict who has engaged in compulsive sexual behaviours to the point of powerlessness, uncontrollability, and extreme dopamine dependence.

Similar to this, not everyone who drinks becomes an alcoholic, therefore they can continue to enjoy their drinking. In contrast, in Russia, the prevalence is 4.7%, nearly 1 in 20 individuals today battle with alcoholism, and 1.4% of people globally have a propensity to become alcoholics. In other words, just like an alcoholic, a sex addict cannot enjoy a moderate amount of their fix because by nature they have a severe allergy to lust and acting out behaviours.

Some people, particularly those who do not have sexual partners, may be asking how masturbation relates to the idea of sexual sobriety. It is confusing since there is a lack of consistency in recovery groups relating to the conduct of masturbating. Compulsive masturbation can become a strongly reinforced behaviour for the majority of sex addicts and is essential to the addictive cycle. Masturbation nearly always involves fantasising and entertaining lustful thoughts or images, which for a sex addict can escalate into an out-of-control compulsive downward spiral with eventual full-blown acting out. This is particularly more challenging if viewing porn while masturbating. From this perspective, it might be critical to acknowledge that masturbation is neither sobriety-friendly nor negotiable for a person in sex addiction recovery. Masturbation is categorically forbidden in some 12-step programs like SA (Sexaholics Anonymous) and doing so is viewed as a violation of sobriety.

There are several crucial considerations that those who support this behaviour during recovery ignore:

- What possible causes or triggers could be behind the urge to masturbate?
- Is the person avoiding the partner by isolating themselves?
- Is it being driven by anything besides sexual desires, such as boredom, anxiety, anger, loneliness, or sense of loss?

These questions, together with the motivation for the want to masturbate, can be signs that the individual is still fighting against recovery rather than surrendering into it.

Research has found that compulsive masturbation dramatically reduces the penis' sensitivity during relational intercourse. Furthermore, numerous recent research has linked excessive masturbation to a variety of negative outcomes, such as interpersonal conflicts, social phobia, social anxiety, stress, episodic panic attacks, high anxiety, depressive episode, decreased relational satisfaction, and the emergence of sex addiction (compulsive sexual behaviours). Recently, the compulsive sexual behaviour disorder (CSBD), which is characterised by a chronic pattern of inability to control intense, repeated sexual urges and behaviours (such as excessive masturbation), was added to the eleventh edition of the International Classification of Diseases (ICD-11).

The basis of sexual sobriety is the desire to manage one's sexual urge in a safe, effective, and healthy way. This can entail postponing sexual activity until an emotional bond has been established with a primary partner. Being sober implies that you don't hold any sexual secrets.

Why Boundaries?

Sobriety is not the same as abstinence. Although, abstinence is a component of sobriety, sobriety also entails a lot more than merely stopping inappropriate sexual behaviour. Relatedly, abstinence is insufficient since it does not provide a substitute for acting out behaviours that enables one to face and deal with life in a healthy manner.

If you are ready for the true definition of a **holistic sobriety** here it is:

To maintain sobriety, you must adopt a holistic perspective that considers your head, eyes, mouth, heart, soul and body.

- **Sobriety in your head-** stay sober in your thoughts. Stop masturbating in your head or harbouring resentment. This is a mental state of sobriety.
- **Sobriety in your eyes-** guarding your eyes and preventing wandering eyes. Stop capturing images to use later.
- **Sobriety in your mouth and language-** stop flirting or approval seeking conversations. Stop using your mouth as a grooming tool.
- **Sobriety in your heart-** avoid becoming better at deception just to become a phoney sober sex addict and instead have a sober heart that is sincere about the recovery process without dishonesty.
- **Sobriety in your soul-** seek to undergo surrendering processes to free your soul from ego and self-centredness.
- **Sobriety in your physicality-** avoid physically acting out behaviours with self or others.

Sexual addiction is by its own nature deceitful, manipulative, self-centred, and it frequently hides behind intellectual justification to support the addict's ego-driven needs. However, in order to maintain sobriety, one must be brutally honest with both oneself and their inner sex addict. Even if you carry yourself subtly while still feeding the addict inside of you, you may no longer be sober. If, for instance, you can discern your true sex addict's intentions only by walking into an adult store, you may have lost your sobriety. You may have lost your sobriety if you are cruising outside a massage parlour without ever stepping inside. Do these examples sound extreme?

Sex addiction is a complex condition and an extreme brain disease that necessitates extreme measures. Furthermore, you are well aware by this point that any covert behaviour that feeds lust will eventually result in a full pledge acting out. Consider all the times you believed you had the upper hand only to discover that you didn't because your addiction had the upper hand. If you want true recovery there is no room for 'but' or excuses; instead, you must be ready to undergo a transformational change since the purpose of sobriety is to replace your old, addictive way of life with a new one. Abstinence won't make you into an admirable person or entirely get rid of the selfish and unpleasant tendencies that make up your character. If you merely concentrate on refraining from acting out when recovering from a sex addiction, you will fail to address the underlying issues that lead to your addiction in the first place. In fact, when someone quits acting out or using the same old coping mechanisms, the negative feelings, inclinations, relational and character defects could intensify. Sex addicts may act out for a variety of reasons, including to escape, anxiety management, dull feelings, relaxation, as a reward, or just for comfort.

After compulsive sexual behaviour ceases, the most efficient coping mechanism (sex addiction) is abolished, leaving the individuals without the necessary healthy resources and skills to deal with challenges and pressures in their lives. Consequently, in order to avoid the reality of their poorly controlled emotions and lives, these individuals instead of acting out turn to dishonesty, additional deceit, rudeness, judgmental attitude, hostility, compulsive overeating or drinking, obsessive shopping, gaming, co-dependency or even fake sobriety. Sobriety contains and necessitates a plan for individual and social growth and wholeness. If you are merely abstaining from acting out behaviours and not actively honouring your holistic sobriety, you cannot benefit from true recovery.

Boundaries and Sobriety

As was previously indicated, a solid sobriety plan with distinct boundaries is necessary for effective recovery. Some sexual sobriety plans have boundaries that are so distinct that they can be considered almost black and white leaving no room for any potential manipulation. These more personal and recovery-related boundaries may evolve over time and become even more specific as the recovering person grows in awareness of their addiction.

If there are no defined boundaries, the sex addict is left exposed to making snap decisions about what is best for them. Unfortunately, most addicts do not make snap decisions that are consistent with their long-term objectives and beliefs. No matter the situation or temporary rationale, the boundaries that comprise the sexual or sobriety plan ensure a safe focus on recovery choices. You should be reminded that the sobriety plan is created once self-disclosure has taken place.

In creating a written description of what sexual sobriety means to them, recovering sex addicts make sure they are explicit about the behaviours that are and are not acceptable. After creating this well-documented and extremely individual concept of sexual sobriety plan, addicts must next commit to honour their new principles. In order to do this, it is suggested that they additionally develop a three-tiered sexual boundary plan with internal, middle, and external or outer boundary that will give them additional and far more comprehensive guidance than a straightforward explanation of what constitutes sexual sobriety.

The outside boundary is living a healthy, happy life whereas the inner boundary is abstaining from certain things and the middle boundary is exercising caution. In the end, sexual boundary strategies involve more than merely abstaining from bottom line and intoxicated behaviours. Despite the fact that this is the fundamental goal, staying sober necessitates much more than simply squirming your way over to the inner boundary.

The Inner Circle Boundaries

Included in this boundary as their non-sober behaviours are the sexual activities that are creating problems in the addict's life. This boundary lists all inappropriate and hazardous sexual behaviours that can lead to unfavourable outcomes, great shame, and a debilitating sense of hopelessness for the addict.

By engaging in one of these actions, the addict is not sexually sober. Please be aware that if, based on your own sex addiction cycle and history, even seemingly subdued behaviours like visiting a brothel without participating, entertain lustful fantasies or flirting online are harmful to your recovery, you may need to include these behaviours in the inner boundary as well.

The inner circle frequently lists the following items:

- Online or offline pornography consumption.
- Compulsive masturbation.

- Webcam sexual activity engagement.
- Using dating websites, social media, or other hook-up apps.
- Engaging with prostitutes or other pay-for-sex practises.
- Casual and/or anonymous sexual encounters.
- Sexting.
- Having affairs.
- Sexual massage.
- Infidelity (cheating on a long-term partner or a spouse).
- Combining sexual activity with drug or alcohol use.
- Exhibitionism comprises of exposing the genitalia in order to stimulate one's sexual arousal or having a strong desire to gain attention from others.
- Voyeurism enjoying oneself sexually while observing others perform sexual acts.
- Masochistic sex taking pleasure in the pain and cruelty inflicted on them by the other person.
- Sadistic sex person purposefully inflicts pain on another for sexual enjoyment.
- Bestiality a human engages in sexual activity with an animal.

The Middle Circle Boundaries

This boundary includes a list of problematic attitudes, behaviours, and circumstances that could push a sex addict back to their inner boundary and relapse. Personal shortcomings and character defects may be placed here if they are still present and not fully unaddressed. The things that could make you want to engage in sexual behaviours outside of the middle border include thoughts, emotions, people, locations, and activities.

While certain problems, like surfing the web for any reason, are evident, others are less so, such as mental or physical tiredness, inadequate sleep, etc., which can lead to anger and increased anxiety, which in turn can then lead to a desire to act out. Again, it may be necessary to mention the indulgence of lustful thoughts and images, covert flirtation, and wandering eyes may need to be placed here.

The middle circle frequently lists the following items:

- Lying and deceptive behaviours.
- Ignoring therapy.
- Flirting.
- Inconsistent attendance to a 12 step recovery meeting.
- Boredom, unstructured time spent alone and or loneliness.
- Argumentative attitude.
- Relational conflicts.
- Poorly managed anxious anger, undefined anger, or resentment.
- Depression.
- Indulging in lust.
- Anxiety.
- Poor self-care.
- Excessive drinking, gaming or watching triggering TV programs.
- Poorly managed emotional dysregulation.
- Acting in behaviours.

The Outer Circle Boundaries

This circle includes a list of positive actions and endeavours that can and ought to help a sex addict in achieving their life goals, which could include leading a positive, healthy sexual life. Addicts who desire to

Why Boundaries?

cease engaging in inappropriate sexual behaviours might switch to these beneficial routines. Furthermore, these boundaries include constructive behaviours that addicts can use when they feel triggered.

Recovery is about replacing unhealthy, destructive addicted behaviours with productive ones. Therefore, if you are not doing recovery, rest assured that you are still doing sex addiction. Your outer circle needs to be made up of routines, actions, and pursuits that support a healthy lifestyle and brain reconditioning.

Over time, your life may gradually become peaceful, liberated, and joyful as a result of these healthy engagements.

The outer circle frequently lists the following items:

- Therapy.
- Spending quality time with family and friends that support sobriety.
- Partaking in healthy hobbies.
- Self-Care.
- Exercise, a nutritious diet, good sleeping practises, etc.
- Developing and increasing one's spirituality.
- Engaging in academic study.
- Participate in a 12-step program.
- In recovery meetings, getting mentorship and helping others.
- Participation in faith based communities and activities.
- Reconnecting with partner and children.
- Completing unfinished home improvement projects.

PRACTICAL RECOVERY TOOLS

Forming Boundaries:

- **Determining what constitutes a boundary-** discover your boundaries and what you should avoid in the early stages of your recovery with the help of your therapist and your network of supporters, even if you don't want to. Describe your needs clearly and honestly here. Your therapist will work with you to determine which triggers are in your control and which are not in order to assist you in correctly adapting your boundaries.
- **Setting boundaries and enforcing them** - establish sobriety friendly boundaries with the aid of a therapist and other supportive individuals. Start by stating your boundaries clearly to both yourself and others. This could seem unusual at the beginning of recovery, especially if you experience shame or low self-worth, but it is a necessary step. However, you can make boundaries, but they won't work if you don't apply them. It takes integrity and dedication every day to uphold them.
- **Sobriety risk factors-** being honest with yourself about the things that put your sobriety in danger will help you identify sobriety risk factors. Your unique sobriety plan may involve both overt and covert risks for you.

- **Accountability-** to maintain healthy boundaries, you must be honest with others about your plan of action. This might be a therapist, a support system, a family member, or a sponsor.
- **Honour others' boundaries** - respect others the way you want to be respected. It's just as important to respect other people's boundaries as it is to uphold your own. It doesn't matter if your boundaries don't match theirs.

Sobriety or Sexual Plan

A future individual sobriety or sexual plan must be in place after a safe disclosure has been conducted. It is critical to recognise your compulsive sexual behaviours right away and on a regular basis. Develop your individual lists of three different types of behaviours in 3 circles. **Complete figure 2:**

Inner circle behaviours (also known as bottom line or addicted behaviours) are those you choose to avoid because they are inherently harmful to your sobriety.

Middle circle behaviours include acting in behaviours and engaging in ways that can lead to the inner circle (for example, indulging lustful fantasies, viewing online adverts, and isolating oneself).

Outer circle behaviours include self-care activities that bring the fulfilment that addicts expected acting out to provide but never did. These are the meaningful activities that replace acting out as the addict learns to take care of themselves and enjoy life. Reading, cycling, physical activities, meditation, prayers, art, playing an instrument, serving, and mentoring are just a few of the things you can do.

⑦ My Inner Circle (Acting Out or Addictive Behaviours)

_____

_____

_____

_____

_____

_____

_____

_____

_____

_____

_____

Why Boundaries?

? My Middle Circle (Risky or Acting In Behaviours)

⁇ My Outer Circle (Self- Care)

___

___

___

___

___

___

⁇ What can you do when becoming aware that you are in your middle circle?

___

___

___

___

___

Why Boundaries?

Figure 3, Print and use to identify the content of your circles

Boundary and Sobriety Question:

⑦ What drives you to establish boundaries?

_____

_____

_____

_____

⁇ What Sexual, physical, relational, emotional and spiritual boundaries did you violate in the past? Explain.

_____

_____

_____

_____

⁇ In comparison to your former habits, how will your new boundaries help you maintain your sobriety?

_____

_____

_____

_____

⁇ Does saying 'no' make you feel bad or like you're disappointing people?

_____

_____

Why Boundaries?

_____

_____

⁇ Are you making an effort to appease everyone around you simply to feel needed? What boundaries do you disregard?

_____

_____

_____

_____

⁇ Have you ever fallen rapidly for someone, with somebody you didn't know well or who had previously reunited with you? What boundaries did you disregard?

_____

_____

_____

_____

⁇ Do you or have you ever violated someone else's physical or sexual boundaries?

_____

_____

_____

_____

⁇ Do you or have you ever wanted to please others by acting as though you agree with them?

_____

_____

_____

_____

⁇ Have you ever used manipulation to get what you want? (This will resonate with you if you routinely overstep or push other people's boundaries).

_____

_____

Why Boundaries?

_____

_____

_____

⑦ Identify your own current or past unhealthy boundaries?

_____

_____

_____

_____

⑦ What does a holistic sobriety definition mean to you?

_____

_____

_____

_____

_____

⁇ What is your own individual definition of sobriety?

_____

_____

_____

⁇ Have you discussed all of your high-risk circumstances with your therapist and your peers?

_____

_____

_____

⁇ Do you have plans in place for all potential high-risk circumstances?

_____

_____

_____

Why Boundaries?

⑦ Do you think that, provided you exercise control, you could be able to indulge in a small bit of lust or masturbation after a prolonged period of abstinence? Explain.

_____

_____

_____

_____

_____

⑦ How does having a healthy new lifestyle relate to true sobriety?

_____

_____

_____

_____

_____

_____

CHAPTER 16

Sex Addiction and Other Health Conditions

It's a common misperception that sex addiction is a moral or choice issue and that stopping is all that is necessary to recover from it. Addiction actually changes the brain, and it takes a lot of intentional and ongoing work to overcome it. An imbalance of natural brain chemicals is the root cause of sex addiction.

Serotonin, dopamine, and norepinephrine are examples of neurotransmitters, which are brain chemicals that assist control mood. Excessive stimulation and elevated levels of these chemicals are linked to compulsive sexual behaviour. In addition to altering the brain's chemical balance, compulsive sexual behaviours also affect the brain's neuronal circuits, particularly those in the brain's reward centre. Similar to other addictions, it typically requires more effort and more intense sexual stimulation to sexually feel satisfied or aroused (due to increased tolerance development). There is a higher likelihood of compulsive sexual behaviour in people who have a history of physical or sexual abuse, alcohol or drug abuse, a mood disorder, a gambling or gaming addiction, dysfunctional family structures, or addicted family members.

Sex addiction frequently co-occurs with other mental illnesses and seldom manifests alone. This suggests that there may be a bi-directional relationship between sex addiction and other mental illnesses, where each affects how the other develops.

How can sex addiction contribute to the emergence of mental illness?

The compulsive and repetitive sexual behaviours of the sex addict may also lead to mental health issues. Sex addiction frequently has negative impacts on a person's life, which can develop into other behavioural issues, alcohol and/or substance use as well as mental diseases including depression and anxiety.

Additionally, particularly among female sex addicts, eating disorders are rather common.

- Due to sex addiction, the emotional danger-sensing circuits can go into overdrive, causing people to experience anxiety, depression, and stress even when they aren't acting out.

- The likelihood of social isolation increases as the addict devotes more time to their addiction and finds less interest in other pursuits. It might be challenging to feel pleasure outside of an addiction since the brain's reward circuitry can alter.

- Addiction has serious emotional consequences since it causes the addict to lose self-control, respect for themselves, and stable relationships. Inability to appreciate relational intimacy is a characteristic of sexual addiction as sex is distorted from a relational intimacy to a sexual object experience. As a result, neurochemical depression could arise from a depressed mood. Sex addiction is marked by an inability to manage anxiety and obsessive preoccupations.

- Obsessive thoughts in turn might increase anxiety. Anxious thoughts in sexual addiction may be preoccupations with the anticipated arousal or thoughts about shame and the unworthy self. When the neurochemistry becomes addiction-oriented, which can intensify anxiety, it is more difficult to unwind and relax in healthy ways.

- Addiction in general is frequently an attempt to address daily challenges in an unhealthy way. Sexual addiction is similar to other addictions and functions as a maladaptive coping mechanism when it comes to handling interpersonal conflicts or inability to control emotional distress. Co-occurring illnesses and sex addiction are quite prevalent because alternative compulsive behaviours, such as gaming, gambling, alcohol or drug use, can be used as a second line of defence against everyday challenges.

- Not to mention, an addict may feel or imagine pressure to fulfill a sexual fantasy as a way to take control of their environment or as a way to escape emotional pain or distress leading to the development of disordered eating or negative body image issues.

How mental or physical illnesses can contribute to the emergence of sex addiction?

A history of mental illness may increase a person's vulnerability to sex addiction.

- Depression or anxiety have been shown to trigger sex addiction. A sense of entitlement to pleasure or a need to exert control may drive one to engage in sexual behaviour, which is also frequently misused as a coping mechanism for anxiety. In this instance, sexual activity is an unhelpful coping mechanism used to try to deal with mental distress and low mood.

- ADHD/ADD, bipolar disorder, autism, obsessive compulsive behaviours (OCD), and delayed cognitive development are just a few of the mental health disorders that can contribute to sex addiction. For example, having ADHD/ ADD, OCD or bipolar disorder make it more difficult for a person to control their impulses, find fulfilment in life, and experiences more anxiety or depression.

- The brain can also be impacted by several medical conditions. Epilepsy, Multiple Sclerosis (MS), and dementia are a few conditions or health issues that may impair the areas of the brain that control sexual behaviours.

- Some dopamine agonist drugs used to treat Parkinson's disease may result in compulsive sexual behaviours.

Sex Addiction and Other Health Conditions

- Autism impairs a person's capacity for accurate reading, appropriate responses, and creation of typical social behaviours. Because of the potential difficulties in emotionally invested relationships, pornography, for instance, offers an appealing sexual outlet.

- Dual diagnoses could be another link between sex addiction and mental health. A person has a dual diagnosis if they struggle with sex addiction as well as one or more mental illnesses. It's crucial to get both diagnosed because each illness affects the other. Obtaining that dual diagnosis is crucial for therapy purposes. If the mental illness and sex addiction are not treated simultaneously, future problems may occur. Although sex addiction can co-occur with mental illnesses, the term 'dual diagnosis' is more frequently used to describe mental illness along with a drug or alcohol use disorder. Similar to drug or alcohol abuse, untreated mental illness can lead to sexual self-medication. It stands to reason that hypersexual behaviour/sex addiction is likely a sign of or consequences of a mental illness, such as adult bipolar disorder, OCD, ADHD/ADD, and other conditions.

For the best chance of overcoming sex addiction, a thorough examination for other mental illnesses is always required. Failure to do so puts the likelihood of effective recovery at risk. The journey will become riddled with difficult and unexpected relapses or fake sobriety.

Sex addiction is frequently viewed as selfish behaviour or as an excuse for inappropriate conduct. Nevertheless, it's worth remembering that sex addiction is an extremely serious problem for many people, regardless of whether it is categorised as a psychiatric illness, a behavioural addiction, or neither.

Dr. Fai Seyed Aghamiri

Pharmacophobia among some sex addicts

Some recovering sex addicts need to combine therapy interventions with either short-term or long-term pharmacological treatments. The fear or scepticism of pharmacological (medical) interventions is especially widespread among sex addicts. Pharmacophobia is the term used to describe the irrational fear of taking medication or committing to any type of medical treatment. This mindset may have its roots in the distorted beliefs and thoughts that characterise all forms of addiction. Pharmacophobics regard drug use negatively, which can lead to ineffective medication use, a complete lack of medication consumption, and a relapse of a condition or illness, all of which have a negative impact on a person's quality of life. Studies have shown that pharmacophobics are more likely to mistrust medical treatments and professionals. Pharmacophobic sex addicts' most common argument is that the medications have too many side effects and could eventually be harmful to their health. However, research shows that pharmacophobics are more likely to have anxiety and personality disorders. For example, since insulin not only improves a diabetic's quality of life but also protects them from a number of harmful health impacts, they are willing to take it for the rest of their lives because it doesn't make sense for them to have an irrational fear of it. According to brain scans, compulsive sexual behaviour has seriously harmed a sex addict's brain in ways comparable to the structural harm experienced by heroin users. Consequently, in order for the brain to perform at its best, there are severe chemical imbalances in the brain that must be corrected. Additionally, underlying physical or mental disorders must, if necessary, be treated pharmacologically. However, Pharmacophobic sex addicts continue to be afraid of receiving what, in some cases, may be their only option for giving their brains what it can no longer give itself.

PRACTICAL RECOVERY TOOLS

Pharmaceuticals intended to treat compulsive sexual behaviours are frequently used as treatment for other disorders. Examples comprise of:

- Antidepressants for the treatment of depression, anxiety, or OCD.

- Naltrexone (Vivitrol), which blocks the area of the brain that experiences pleasure from some addictive behaviours, is typically used to treat alcohol and opiate dependency. With behavioural addictions like compulsive sexual behaviours or a gambling addiction, it might be effective.

- Mood stabilizers may lessen compulsive sexual impulses even though they are often used to treat bipolar disorder.

- Anti-androgen medications reduce the biological effects of androgens (sex hormones) on males. Men who engage in dangerously compulsive sexual behaviours are routinely prescribed anti-androgens because they suppress sexual urges.

Sexual Addiction and Related Mental and Physical Illness Questions:

Please share your responses to the following questions with your therapist and, if required, a medical professional for additional evaluation.

⁇ How frequently do you experience anxiety and nervousness?

_____

_____

_____

_____

⁇ How frequently do you feel so anxious that nothing can make you feel better or clam down?

_____

_____

_____

_____

Sex Addiction and Other Health Conditions

⑦ How do you feel hopeless, and under what circumstances?

_____

_____

_____

_____

_____

⑦ How frequently do you feel fidgety or restless?

_____

_____

_____

_____

⑦ How often do you feel depressed?

_____

_____

_____

_____

⁉ How frequently do you feel unable to sit still due to restlessness?

_____

_____

_____

_____

⁉ How often do you feel like everything is a struggle or an effort?

_____

_____

_____

_____

⁉ How frequently do you feel so depressed that nothing can make you feel better?

_____

_____

_____

_____

Sex Addiction and Other Health Conditions

⑦ How frequently do you feel unworthy, and under what circumstances?

_____

_____

_____

_____

⑦ After the difficult aspects of a job are finished, how frequently do you struggle to finish the last few details?

_____

_____

_____

_____

⑦ How frequently do you find it difficult to organise yourself when you have to complete a task?

_____

_____

⑦ How often do you struggle to recall duties or appointments?

⑦ Do you avoid or put off starting a task that needs a lot of consideration?

? How often do you make huge mistakes while working on a time-consuming or difficult assignment?

_____
_____
_____
_____

? How frequently do you find it difficult to focus on what people are saying to you, even when they are speaking directly to you?

_____
_____
_____
_____

? Do you find it tough to wait your turn when it's necessary?

_____
_____
_____
_____

⑦ During a conversation, do you ever find yourself completing people's sentences before they can finish them on their own?

_____

_____

_____

_____

⑦ Do you ever feel so happy or pumped up that you make other people question your normal self or are so pumped up that you end up in trouble?

_____

_____

_____

⑦ Have you ever had your drinking, gaming, gambling, excessive use of technology, or drug use criticised?

_____

_____

Sex Addiction and Other Health Conditions

⓶ Do you hesitate or worry about taking medication?

⓶ What is your possible justification for your drug-phobia or fear?

⓶ What is the evidence that your drug-phobia may be real?

⑦ In the absence of medication, how do you propose to properly treat your physical or mental condition?

⑦ Do you know how effectively, you might treat your mental or physical illness without using any medication?

CHAPTER 17

Recovery in a Nutshell

The next step is to create your personal recovery plan when you have established all of your circles. Your recovery plan should specify the exact steps you'll take to improve your physical and mental health, make amends with those your sex addiction has harmed, prevent any relapse, especially before and during cravings, and more.

Your recovery plan includes all of your own boundaries, dos and don'ts, and acting in or acting out behaviours. You might want to avoid certain individuals, locations, and circumstances in order to reduce your risk of relapsing. There is no way to completely avoid high-risk individuals or circumstances, but you can be aware of your own triggers and try to stay away from them as much as you can. This is not the time to test yourself.

Create a strategy so that you can deal with cravings if they appear. If you know in advance that you will be in a potentially risky situation. If you find yourself in a scenario that triggers or tempts you EXIT even if it means you may offend some people because your recovery must come FIRST.

Find your supportive people to talk to about how you're feeling and keep a daily journal about your feelings. When you try to reach someone by phone, but they are not accessible, you text your entire inner circle of five people, and before you know it, calls start coming in. Plan ahead with your supportive circle of five people to send an S.O.S. if you need to contact them right away. Send the text to all of them so you may get as much support as you can, especially if you've had persistent triggers or are on the verge of relapsing. Apart from SA meetings, You must go to AA, and NA, if you are also addicted to alcohol or drugs.

Read recovery material, such as the A.A. Big Book, SA literature etc, since it might motivate you, offer some helpful advice, and possibly ease your anxiety.

With the aid of committed support and thoughtful preparation, being exposed to craving circumstances while abstaining can aid in reducing or eliminating triggers.

During recovery, sex addicts have a lot of negative emotions. Their addiction has largely disturbed and, in some cases, destroyed their and others' lives – spouses, friends, and families have been torn apart, and livelihoods have been harmed. Additionally, Addicts carry uncomfortable feelings with themselves for causing such a shambles, at their parents for their lack of nurturing and setting them up for failure, and at the world for refusing to give them a break. Addicts are conditioned to fear their uncomfortable feelings as a result of their addiction, making acting out sexually the only way they are capable to control and numb them. Through therapy, journaling about your feelings, and regularly sharing with your supportive network, you will have a healthy avenue to express your unpleasant emotions.

Recovery means learning from a lapse or a relapse

A slip-up or relapse can occasionally be a necessary component of a successful recovery if the experience is used as a teaching opportunity to avoid similar mistakes in the future and to strengthen sobriety. If you make a mistake, you can learn from it as follows:

1. **LEAVE THE SITUATION.** The longer you stay in a high-risk scenario, the more impaired your judgement will get, the more you'll entertain lust the more difficult it will be to see things clearly.
2. **LEARN FROM THE SLIP OR RELAPSE.** The fact that the slip occurred shows that you either miscalculated or need more insight in how to avoid future risks. You're not a failure if you make a mistake; it just means you need to make a better plan for your addiction and yourself.
3. **INVESTIGATE.** Identify your triggers, vulnerabilities, and actions even a few days before a lapse or relapse. Did you make any poor decisions that increased risk, such as being complacent or giving in to lust? Did you successfully deal with any negative emotions or thoughts prior to the slip? Has your way of life aided your recovery, or do you need to make some changes?
4. **DISCLOSE THE LAPSE OR RELAPSE WITH SUPPORTIVE PEOPLE.** This could lead to more acting out or even bingeing, and it will encourage more dishonest behaviour. Having an honest discussion with others might provide you further context for the relapse.

5. **CREATE A PREVENTION PLAN.** Make a decision in advance regarding what you would do differently the next time to prevent the same mistakes in order to decrease or eliminate the possibility of a full-blown relapse.

PRACTICAL RECOVERY TOOLS

Sex addiction therapy.

- Utilize one or more trigger management strategies to prevent entertaining lust (i.e., snapping your rubber band, counting backwards form 100 to 0, recite a bible verse or prayer, make a call to a supportive accountability person etc).
- Identify your HALT.
- Protect your eyes.
- Commit to rigorous honesty.
- Attend meetings regularly – peer groups are advantageous because they make people feel less alone, teach them what the voice of addiction sounds like by hearing it in others, teach them how other people have handled recovery and what coping mechanisms have worked, and provide a safe environment where they won't be judged.
- Engage in step work.

- Create a daily phone program by starting a live call with your support system, including your sponsor and circle of five supportive individuals.
- Journaling and positive self-talk.
- Read and write positive literature.
- Early in the morning, say a 30-second prayer for a sober day, and another for thanksgiving at bedtime.
- Daily meditation.
- Develop a healthy network of relationships and engage with sobriety friendly individuals.
- Read and revise your circles and boundaries every day.
- Self-care.
- Physical exercise- exercise regularly 3-4 times weekly to reduce tension.
- Surrender to your recovery, therapy, and your powerlessness to lust.
- Identify your acting in behaviours and continuously work to address them.
- Create a culture of gratitude and appreciation.
- Look to increase your spiritual awareness to give life meaning and connect with the God of your understanding.
- Keep your home space free from all types of adult (sexual) material.
- Use self-affirmations to start each day, such as 'I choose to maintain sobriety and surrender my character defects.'
- Maintain healthy nutrition by avoiding concentrated sweets and eating three well-balanced meals per day.
- Balance work and play.
- Make recovery a daily priority.
- Learn from past slip ups but do not repeat them.

Recovery Questions:

⑦ Give some particular instances that pose a high risk to your recovery.

_____

_____

_____

_____

⑦ Give some examples of your previous coping mechanisms for handling the circumstances in the previous question?

_____

_____

_____

_____

⑦ Determine the effects of these previous behaviours?

_____

_____

Recovery in a Nutshell

_____

_____

_____

⑦ Describe the result you are seeking for your own recovery.

_____

_____

_____

_____

⑦ Describe your new plan of action to get the desired results in your recovery?

_____

_____

_____

_____

? Describe the advantages you expect your new sober practices will provide?

_____
_____
_____
_____

? What coping mechanisms do you employ when under stress?

_____
_____
_____
_____

? Are you considerably nervous or depressed?

_____
_____
_____
_____

? What activities do you enjoy engaging in to fulfill your intellectual curiosity?

_____
_____
_____
_____

? Do you regularly engage in creative or artistic pursuits? Explain.

_____
_____
_____
_____

? What skills or talents do you have that you're not using to your best potential?

_____
_____
_____
_____

⁇ Are your interactions with family members generally satisfying?

⁇ How much time do you spend with your family?

⁇ Can you count on your family for support and assistance?

ⓘ How are the amount and quality of the relationships in your personal life?

_____

_____

_____

_____

ⓘ Who among your friends can you rely on for assistance and support?

_____

_____

_____

_____

ⓘ When and how do you communicate your needs, wants, and emotions to other people?

_____

_____

_____

(?) Describe any particular relationships that you have serious problems with?

(?) Is your life filled with enough love? Explain.

(?) Do you experience inner tranquillity? Explain.

_____

_____

(?) What are the ways in which you attend to your spiritual life?

_____

_____

_____

_____

(?) Do you put too much time or effort into your work? Explain.

_____

_____

_____

_____

(?) Generally speaking, how do you feel about your work situation?

_____

_____

⊙ Describe if you currently face any pressing financial issues?

⊙ Describe your approach to wise financial management?

⊙ What have you learned from your past lapses or relapses?

? What elements of your recovery strategy have proven to be the most valuable tools?

? Five years from now, where would you be in terms of your recovery and life?

Dr. Fai Seyed Aghamiri

Please go to this link https://tinyurl.com/PDFworkbook to download your PDF workbook.

References

Alcoholics Anonymous World Services. *Alcoholics Anonymous Big Book* (4th ed.). (2002).

Aldwin, C. M., Park, C. L., Jeong, Y., & Nath, R. (2014). Differing pathways between religiousness, spirituality, and health: A self-regulation perspective. *Psychology of Religion and Spirituality*, 6(1), 9-21. https://doi.org/10.1037/a0034416

American Psychiatric Association.(1987) Diagnostics and statistical manual of mental disorders. 3rd ed, rev. Washington, DC: American Psychiatric Press.

American Psychological Association. (2009) *APA Concise Dictionary of Psychology*. Washington, DC: American Psychological Association.

Argo, C. (2018). *Awaken & Grow: A Practical Guide For Your Spiritual Journey*. Haldi Press.

B, Liu Y, Cascio C, Wang Z, Insel TR. (2000), Dopamine D2 receptors in the nucleus accumbens are important for social attachment in female prairie voles (Microtus ochrogaster). Behav Neurosci.114(1):173-83. Doi: 10.1037//0735-7044.114.1.173. PMID: 10718272.

Bandura, A. (1994). Self-Efficacy. In R. J. Corsini (Ed.), *Encyclopedia of psychology (2nd ed., Vol. 3, pp. 368-369)*. New York, NY: Wiley.

Bandura, A. (1997). Behavior theory and the models of man (1974). In J. M. Notterman (Ed.), *The evolution of psychology: Fifty years of the American psychologist (pp. 154–172)*. Washington, DC: American Psychological Association.

Bandura, A. (2001). Social cognitive theory: An agentic perspective. *Annual Review of Psychology, 52(1)*, 1-26.

Bandura, A. (2008). An agentic perspective on positive psychology. In S. J. Lopez (Ed.), Praeger perspectives. *Positive psychology: Exploring the best in people (Vol. 1., pp. 167–196)*. Westport, CT: Praeger Publishers/ Greenwood Publishing Group

Baumeister, R. F., Bratslavsky, E. (1999). Passion, intimacy, and time: Passionate love as a function of change in intimacy. Personality and Social Psychology Review, 3, 49–67. doi:10.1207/s15327957pspr0301_3 Google Scholar | SAGE Journals

Beris, R. (2013). Science Says Silence is Much More Important to Our Brains than We Think. Geraadpleegd van http://www. lifehack. org/377243/ science-says-silence-much-more-important-our-brains-than-thought.

Berridge, K.C., (2012) From Prediction Error to Incentive Salience: Mesolimbic Computation of Reward Motivation. European Journal Neuroscience, 35(7),1124-1143. https://doi.org/10.1111/j.1460-9568.2012.07990.x

Boelens PA, Reeves RR, Replogle WH, Koenig HG. (2009). A randomized trial of the effect of prayer on depression and anxiety. International journal of psychiatry in medicine:39(4),377-92. PMID: https://doi.org/10.2190/PM.39.4.c, 20391859.

Breland-Noble, A. M., Wong, M. J., Childers, T., Hankerson, S., & Sotomayor, J. (2015). Spirituality and religious coping in African

References

American youth with depressive illness. *Mental health, religion & culture*, 18(5), 330–341. https://doi.org/10.1080/13674676.2015.1056120

Carnes, P. (1983) *Out of the Shadows: Understanding Sexual Addiction.* Minneapolis: CompCare Publishers.

Carnes, P. (1989) *Contrary to Love: Helping the Sexual Addict.* Minneapolis: CompCare Publishers, 218-9

Carnes, P. (1991) *Don't Call it Love: Recovery from Sexual Addiction.* New York: Bantam Books, 42-4

Colman, A. M.(2006). *Oxford Dictionary of Psychology.* New York, NY: Oxford University Press.

Coleman, E. (1990) The obsessive-compulsive model for describing compulsive sexual behaviour. *American journal of preventative psychiatry and neurology*, 2(3)9-14

Corneille, J. S., & Luke, D. (2021). Spontaneous spiritual awakenings: phenomenology, altered states, individual differences, and well-being. *Frontiers in psychology*, *12*, 720579. https://DOI/10.3389/fpsyg.2021.720579

Daghestani, A. N. (1987). Why should physicians recognize compulsive gambling? *Postgraduate Medicine, 82*(5), 253–263. https://doi.org/10.1080/00325481.1987.11700012

Eagleman, D., (2015) *The Brain: The Story of You.* Pantheon Books

Esch, T., & Stefano, G. B. (2011). The neurobiological link between compassion and love. *Medical Science Monitor, 17*(3), RA65–RA75. https://doi.org/10.12659/msm.881441

Falchuk. A. (2016). *Why Surrender.* https://goop.com/wellness/mindfulness/why-surrender/

Fisher, H., Aron, A., & Brown, L. L. (2005). Romantic love: An fMRI study of a neural mechanism for mate choice. *The Journal of Comparative Neurology, 493*(1), 58–62. https://doi.org/10.1002/cne.20772

Fleming, A., (2015) The Science of Craving. Intelligent Life, May/June. http://moreintelligentlife.com/content/features/wanting-versus-liking

Förster, J., Özelsel, A., & Epstude, K. (2010). How love and lust change people's perception of relationship partners. *Journal of Experimental Social Psychology*, 46(2), 237-246, https://doi.org/10.1026/j.jesp.2009.08.009

Fredrickson, B., Prinzing, M., (2020). *How to have a better day during the pandemic.* College of Arts and Sciences. https://college.unc.edu/2020/06/how-to-have-a-better-day-during-the- pandemic/

Galanter, M. (2016). *What Is Alcoholics Anonymous? A Path from Addiction to Recovery.* Oxford University Press.

Garland, E. L., & Howard, M. O. (2018). Mindfulness-based treatment of addiction: current state of the field and envisioning the next wave of research. *Addiction Science & Clinical Practice*, 13(1). https://doi.org/10.1186/s13722-018-0115-3

Gazerani, P. (2017). Pharmacophobia and pharmacophilia in analgesic use. *Pain Management*, 7(5), 341–344. https://doi.org/10.2217/pmt-2017-0015

Goodman A. (1989). Addiction defined: diagnostic criteria for addictive disorder. Am J Prev Psychiatry Nuerol;2(1):12-5

Grubbs JB, Kraus SW, Perry SL.(2019). Self-reported addiction to pornography in a nationally representative sample: The roles of use habits, religiousness, and moral incongruence. J Behav Addict. Mar 1;8(1):88-93. doi: 10.1556/2006.7.2018.134. Epub Jan 11. PMID: 30632378; PMCID: PMC7044607.

Harvard Help Guide. (2022). *Understanding Addiction.* HelpGuide.org. https://www.helpguide.org/harvard/how-addiction-hijacks-the-brain.htm

Shi, W., He, X., Han, X., Wang, N., Zhang, N., & Wang, X. (2015). The interventional effects of loving-kindness meditation on positive emotions and interpersonal interactions. *Neuropsychiatric Disease and Treatment*, 1273. https://doi.org/10.2147/ndt.s79607

References

Heatherton T. F. (2011). Neuroscience of self and self-regulation. *Annual review of psychology*, *62*, 363–390. https://doi.org/10.1146/annurev.psych.121208.131616

Heatherton, T. F., & Wagner, D. D. (2011). Cognitive neuroscience of self-regulation failure. *Trends in Cognitive Sciences*, *15*(3), 132–139. https://doi.org/10.1016/j.tics.2010.12.005

Hopkin, M. (2004). Link proved between senses and memory. *Nature*. https://doi.org/10.1038/news040524-12

Jans-Beken, L., Lataster, J., Leontjevas, R., & Jacobs, N. (2015). Measuring gratitude: A comparative validation of the Dutch Gratitude Questionnaire (GQ6) and Short Gratitude, Resentment, and Appreciation Test (SGRAT). *Psychologica Belgica*, *55*(1), 19–31. https://doi.org/10.5334/pb.bd

Jha, A. (2021). *Peak Mind: Find Your Focus, Own Your Attention, Invest 12 Minutes a Day*. Hachette UK.

K, R. (2004). Keys to recovery. https://www.roykfiles.com/surrenderaccountability2004.pdf

Kaplan MS, Krueger RB.(2010)_Diagnosis, assessment, and treatment of hypersexuality. J Sex Res. 2010 Mar;47(2):181-98. doi: 10.1080/00224491003592863. PMID: 20358460.

Karandashev, V. (2015). A cultural perspective on romantic love. *Online Readings in Psychology and Culture*, *5*(4). https://doi.org/10.9707/2307-0919.1135

Khng, K. H. (2017). A better state-of-mind: Deep breathing reduces state anxiety and enhances test performance through regulating test cognitions in children. *Cognition and Emotion*, *31*(7), 1502-1510. https://doi.org/10.1080/02699931.2016.1233095

Kosoglou. A. (2019). 20 Prayers for Addiction Recovery. https://royallifecenters.com/20-prayers-for-addiction-recovery/

Krentzman, A. R. (2019). A full and thankful heart: writings about gratitude by Alcoholics Anonymous co-founder, Bill Wilson. *Addiction*

Research & Theory, 27(6), 451–461. https://doi.org/10.1080/16066359.2018.1547816

Kromer, J., Hummel, T., Pietrowski, D., Giani, A. S., Sauter, J., Ehninger, G., … Croy, I. (2016). Influence of HLA on human partnership and sexual satisfaction. *Scientific Reports, 6*(1). https://doi.org/10.1038/srep32550

Kurniasanti, K. S., Assandi, P., Ismail, R. I., Nasrun, M. W., & Wiguna, T. (2019). Internet addiction: A new addiction? *Medical Journal of Indonesia, 28*(1), 82-91. https://doi.org/10.13181/mji.v28i1.2752

Lange, J., Redford, L., & Crusius, J. (2019). A status-seeking account of psychological entitlement. *Personality and Social Psychology Bulletin, 45*(7), 1113-1128. https://doi.org/10.1177/0146167218808501

Langeslag, S. J., & Van Strien, J. W. (2016). Regulation of romantic love feelings: Preconceptions, strategies, and feasibility. *PLOS ONE, 11*(8), e0161087. https://doi.org/10.1371/journal.pone.0161087

Lassiter, P. S., & Culbreth, J. R. (2017). *Theory and Practice of Addiction Counselling*, Sage Publications.

Lee, H.-G., Kim, Y.-C., Dunning, J. S., & Han, K.-A. (2008). Recurring Ethanol Exposure Induces Disinhibited Courtship in Drosophila. *PLoS ONE, 3*(1), e1391. https://doi.org/10.1371/journal.pone.0001391

Life and Wellness Coaches. (n.d.) WebMD. Accessed February 17, 2015. https://www.webmd.com/balance/guide/life-and-wellness-coaches

Lillo-Crespo, M., Forner-Ruiz, M., Riquelme-Galindo, J., Ruiz-Fernández, D., & García-Sanjuan, S. (2019). Chess practice as a protective factor in dementia. *International Journal of Environmental Research and Public Health, 16*(12), 2116. https://doi.org/10.3390/ijerph16122116

Linn, LS,, Spiegel, J., Mathews, W., et al.(1989), Recent sexual behaviours among homosexual men seeking primary medical care. Arch Intern Med; 149(12):2685-90

References

Litt, A., Khan, U., Shiv, B., (2010) Lusting while loathing: Parallel Counterdriving of wanting and liking. Psychological Science, 21(1): p. 118-125. DOI:10.1177/0956797609355633

Loren, L. D. (2017). *Riding the Roller Coaster: Sequel to Lust, Love, and Obligation.*

Manjaly, Z., Harrison, N. A., Critchley, H. D., Do, C. T., Stefanics, G., Wenderoth, N., Lutterotti, A., Müller, A., & Stephan, K. E. (2019). Pathophysiological and cognitive mechanisms of fatigue in multiple sclerosis. *Journal of Neurology, Neurosurgery & Psychiatry, 90*(6), 642-651. https://doi.org/10.1136/jnnp-2018-320050

McClintock, C. H., Lau, E., & Miller, L. (2016). Phenotypic Dimensions of Spirituality: Implications for Mental Health in China, India, and the United States. *Frontiers in Psychology, 7.* https://doi.org/10.3389/fpsyg.2016.01600

McCullough, M. E., & Willoughby, B. L. B. (2009). Religion, self-regulation, and self-control: Associations, explanations, and implications. *Psychological Bulletin, 135*(1), 69–93. https://doi.org/10.1037/a0014213

Melemis, S. M. (2010). *I Want to Change My Life: How to Overcome Anxiety, Depression, and Addiction.*

Melemis, S.M. (2015). Focus: Addiction: relapse prevention and the five rules of recovery. *The Yale journal of biology and medicine, 88*(3), 325.

Milkman, H.B., Sunderwirth, S.G. (1987) *Craving for Ecstasy: The Consciousness and Chemistry of Escape.* Lexington, MA; Lexington Books:40

Mills, P. J., Redwine, L., Wilson, K., Pung, M. A., Chinh, K., Greenberg, B. H., Lunde, O., Maisel, A., Raisinghani, A., Wood, A., & Chopra, D. (2015). The role of gratitude in spiritual well-being in asymptomatic heart failure patients. *Spirituality in Clinical Practice, 2*(1), 5-17. https://doi.org/10.1037/scp0000050

Mindful. (2022). Here are five reasons to meditate. https://www.mindful.org/how-to-meditate/

Moeller, S. J., Crocker, J., & Bushman, B. J. (2009). Creating hostility and conflict: Effects of entitlement and self-image goals. *Journal of Experimental Social Psychology*, *45*(2), 448-452. https://doi.org/10.1016/j.jesp.2008.11.005

National Highway Traffic Safety Administration. Research on Drowsy Driving. http://www.nhtsa.gov/Driving+Safety/Drowsy+DrivingExternal. Accessed October 20, 2015.

Newberg, A. B. (2013). *The Metaphysical Mind: Probing the Biology of Philosophical Thought*. CreateSpace.

Newberg, A. B. (2014). The neuroscientific study of spiritual practices. *Frontiers in Psychology*, *5*, 215. https://doi.org/10.3389/fpsyg.2014.00215

Norcross, J. C., Krebs, P. M., & Prochaska, J. O. (2011). Stages of change. *Psychotherapy Relationships That Work*, 279-300. https://doi.org/10.1093/acprof:oso/9780199737208.003.0014

od, but love triggers parts of the brain associated with habits.

Okonoda, K. M., & Allagoa, E. L. (2020). Compulsive Sexual Behaviors in a Young Male with Social Anxiety Disorder (Social Phobia). *J Psychiatry*, *23*, 471. doi: 10.35248/2378-5756.20.23.471

Pargament, K. I., Koenig, H. G., Tarakeshwar, N., & Hahn, J. (2004). Religious Coping Methods as Predictors of Psychological, Physical and Spiritual Outcomes among Medically Ill Elderly Patients: A Two-year Longitudinal Study. *Journal of Health Psychology*, *9*(6), 713-730. https://doi.org/10.1177/1359105304045366

Pickard, H. (2016). Denial in addiction. *Mind & Language*, *31*(3), 277-299. https://doi.org/10.1111/mila.12106

Polcin DL, Korcha R, Bond J, Galloway G. (2010). What did we learn from our study on sober living houses and where do we go from here? Journal of

References

Psychoactive Drugs.42(4):425-33. doi: 10.1080/02791072.2010.10400705. PMID: 21305907; PMCID: PMC3057870.

Ram, D. (2017). Family dynamics may influence an individual's substance use abstinence self-efficacy. *Journal of Addiction and Preventive Medicine, 02*(01). https://doi.org/10.19104/japm.2016.106

Ritchie, H., & Roser, M. (2018, April). Alcohol consumption. Retrieved from Our World in Data website: https://ourworldindata.org/alcohol-consumption

Robards J, Evandrou M, Falkingham J, Vlachantoni A. (2012) Marital status, health and mortality. *Maturitas.*73(4):295-299. Doi: 10.1016/j.maturitas.2012.08.007

Roberson, P.N.E., Fincham, F. (2018). Is relationship quality linked to diabetes risk and management? It depends on what you look at. *Families, System & Health,*36(3):315-326. https://doi:10.1037/fsh0000336

Robinson, T. E., & Berridge, K. C. (2008). Review. The incentive sensitization theory of addiction: some current issues. *Philosophical transactions of the Royal Society of London. Series B, Biological sciences, 363*(1507), 3137–3146. https://doi.org/10.1098/rstb.2008.0093

Rubin, Z. (1974). Lovers and other strangers: The development of intimacy in encounters and relationships: Experimental studies of self-disclosure between strangers at bus stops and in airport departure lounges can provide clues about the development of intimate relationships. *American Scientist, 62*(2), 182-190.

Ruiz, M., Mills, J. (1999). *Prayer for self-love.* https://www.thefouragreements.com/prayer-for-self-love/

Salzberg, S. (2020). *Loving kindness: The Revolutionary Art of Happiness.* Shambhala Publications.

Schneider, JP. (1988). *Back from Betrayal: Recovering from his Affairs.* San Francisco: Harper/Hazelden, 26-35

Schneider, JP. (1989). Rebuilding the marriage during recovery from compulsive sexual behavior. *Family Relations*,38, 288-94

Schneider, JP. (1990) Sexual problems in married couples recovering from sexual addiction and addiction. *American journal for preventative psychiatry and neurology*, 2(3):33-8

Schneider, J.P., Schneider, B.H., (1990). Marital satisfaction during recovery from self-identified sexual addiction among bisexual men and their wives. *Journal of sex & marital therapy* 16(4):230-50. https://doi.org/10.1080/00926239008405460

Schneider, J.P., Schneider, B. (1991) *Sex, Lies and Forgiveness: Couples Speaking Out on Healing From Sex Addiction.* Centre City, MN: Hazelden Educational Materials.

Schneiderman, I., Zagoory-Sharon, O., Leckman, J. F., & Feldman, R. (2012). Oxytocin during the initial stages of romantic attachment: relations to couples' interactive reciprocity. *Psychoneuroendocrinology*, *37*(8), 1277–1285. https://doi.org/10.1016/j.psyneuen.2011.12.021

Schnitker, S. A., & Richardson, K. L. (2019). Framing gratitude journaling as prayer amplifies its hedonic and eudaimonic well-being, but not health, benefits. *The Journal of Positive Psychology*, *14*(4), 427-439.

Seshadri, K. G. (2016). The neuroendocrinology of love. *Indian journal of endocrinology and metabolism*, *20*(4), 558–563. https://doi.org/10.4103/2230-8210.183479

Sexaholics Anonymous Statement of Principle. (2016). Why stop lusting? https://www.sa.org/w/wp-content/uploads/whystop.pdf

Sharma, H. (2015). Meditation: Process and effects. *AYU*, *36*(3), 233–237. https://doi.org/10.4103/0974-8520.182756

Shevchuk, N. A. (2008). Adapted cold shower as a potential treatment for depression. *Medical Hypotheses*, *70*(5), 995-1001. https://doi.org/10.1016/j.mehy.2007.04.052

References

Substance Abuse Treatment and Family Therapy. (2004). Substance Abuse and Mental Health Services Administration. December 24, 2014.

Szegedy-Maszak, M. (2005). Mysteries of the mind. *U.S. News World Report, 138*(7), 52–61

Tanyi, R. A. (2002). Towards clarification of the meaning of spirituality. *Journal of Advanced Nursing, 39*(5), 500-509. https://doi.org/10.1046/j.1365-2648.2002.02315.x

Teo, A.R., Choi, H., & Valenstein, M. (2013) Social Relationships and Depression: Ten-Year Follow-Up from a Nationally Representative Study. *PLoS One,* 8(4): e62396. https://doi.org/10.1371/journal.pone.0062396

Timmerman, G. M. (1991). A concept analysis of intimacy. *Issues in mental health nursing, 12*(1), 19–30. https://doi.org/10.3109/01612849109058207

van Lankveld, J., Jacobs, N., Thewissen, V., Dewitte, M., & Verboon, P. (2018). The associations of intimacy and sexuality in daily life: Temporal dynamics and gender effects within romantic relationships. *Journal of Social and Personal Relationships, 35*(4), 557–576, https://doi.org/10.1177/0265407517743076

Verhaeghe, J. Gheysen, R., Enzlin, P.,(2013) Pheromones and their effect on women's mood and sexuality. Facts Views Vis Obgyn, 5(3):189-195.

Washton, A.M.,(1989) Cocaine may trigger sexual compulsivity. US J Drug Alcohol Depend,13(6):8

Weiss, R., Ferree, M. (2018). *Out of the Doghouse for Christian men: A Redemptive Guide for Men Caught Cheating.* Createspace Independent Publishing Platform.

Wellness Society, (2019) *STOP technique.* https://thewellnesssociety.org/wp-content/uploads/2019/02/STOP-Technique-PDF-1.pdf

Withers, A., Zuniga, K., Sell, S., (2017). Spirituality: Concept analysis. *International Journal of Nursing & Clinical Practices, 4(1)* https://doi.org/10.15344/2394-4978/2017/234

Witkiewitz, K., Marlatt, G. A. (2007). Overview of relapse prevention. *Therapist's Guide to Evidence-Based Relapse Prevention*, 3-17. https://doi.org/10.1016/b978-012369429-4/50031-8

Wong, C.W., Kwok, C.S., Narain, A., et al.(2018). Marital status and risk of cardiovascular diseases: a systematic review and meta-analysis. *Heart,* 104(23):1937-1948. doi:10.1136/heartjnl-2018-313005

Zimmer, F., Imhoff, R. (2020). Abstinence from masturbation and hypersexuality. *Archives of Sexual Behavior, 49*(4), 1333-1343 https://doi.org/10.1007/s10508-019-01623-8.

Services and Offers

Sex addiction therapy for individuals and their partners (AASAT; American Association for Sex Addiction Therapy), AASAT Betrayal Partner Recovery Specialist, AASAT Intimacy Anorexia Specialist, Gottman (level 1, 2), NLP, Hypnosis, NeurOptimal® neurofeedback, EMDR, trauma and PTSD management, infidelity recovery, Gestalt therapy, cognitive behavioural therapy, mindfulness practice, betrayal trauma, ADHD, depression and family therapy.

Bonus for finishing this book:
30 minutes free consultation with Dr Fai where you can have all your questions answered in private.

Contact details
Ph. 0413 482 486

www.houseofhopecounsellingcentre.com.au
enquiries@houseofhopecounselling.com.au

Additional Thoughts

www.ingramcontent.com/pod-product-compliance
Lightning Source LLC
Chambersburg PA
CBHW070459120526
44590CB00013B/696